## ALSO BY DAVE BARRY

### FICTION

*Insane City*

*Lunatics* (with Alan Zweibel)

*The Bridge to Never Land* (with Ridley Pearson)

*Peter and the Sword of Mercy* (with Ridley Pearson)

*Science Fair* (with Ridley Pearson)

*Peter and the Secret of Rundoon* (with Ridley Pearson)

*Cave of the Dark Wind* (with Ridley Pearson)

*The Shepherd, the Angel, and Walter the Christmas Miracle Dog*

*Escape from the Carnivale* (with Ridley Pearson)

*Peter and the Shadow Thieves* (with Ridley Pearson)

*Peter and the Starcatchers* (with Ridley Pearson)

*Tricky Business*

*Big Trouble*

### NONFICTION

*Live Right and Find Happiness (Though Beer Is Much Faster)*

*You Can Date Boys When You're 40*

*I'll Mature When I'm Dead*

*Dave Barry's History of the Millennium (So Far)*

*Dave Barry's Money Secrets*

# Dave Barry

# BEST.
# STATE.
# EVER.

## A FLORIDA MAN DEFENDS HIS HOMELAND

G. P. PUTNAM'S SONS · NEW YORK

PUTNAM

G. P. PUTNAM'S SONS
*Publishers Since 1838*
An imprint of Penguin Random House LLC
375 Hudson Street
New York, New York 10014

ISBN 9781101982600

Printed in the United States of America
1   3   5   7   9   10   8   6   4   2

*Book design by Meighan Cavanaugh*

To my fellow Floridians:

Don't ever sober up.

# CONTENTS

# INTRODUCTION

very few months I get a call from some media person wanting to interview me about Florida, where I have lived for three decades. The tone of the interview is never positive, or even neutral. The interviewer never asks: "Why do you live in Florida?" Or: "What do you like about Florida?"

No, the tone is always: "What the hell is *wrong* with Florida?"

I should note that these interviewers are not always calling from states that have a lot to brag about. I have been interviewed on the wrongness of Florida by people who live in, for example, Illinois. Not to be picky, but there are a few things wrong with Illinois. For one thing, the voters there keep electing criminals to high office. Illinois constantly has to build new prisons just to hold all of its convicted former governors, who form violent prison gangs and get into rumbles with gangs of convicted former state legislators. If Charles Manson ever gets out on parole and needs a job, he can move to Illinois and run for governor. The voters would say, "Looks like gubernatorial material to me!"

Also, Illinois has done a poor job of handling its finances, which is why its official credit rating, as determined by Moody's Investors Service, was recently lowered from "Meth Addict" to "Labrador Retriever." And *this* is the state from which a media person called to ask me what is wrong with Florida.

Florida has become The Joke State, the state everybody makes fun of. If states were characters on *Seinfeld*, Florida would be Kramer: Every time it appears, the audience automatically laughs, knowing it's going to do some idiot thing.

We weren't always The Joke State. We used to be The Sunshine State, known for our orange groves and beaches and deceased senior citizens playing shuffleboard. People might have seen Florida as *boring*, but they didn't laugh at it. They laughed at New Jersey, because it contained the New Jersey Turnpike and smelled like a giant armpit. Or they laughed at California, because it was populated by trend-obsessed goobers wearing Earth shoes and getting recreational enemas. Or they laughed at Indiana, because the people there proudly call themselves Hoosiers even though they have no idea what *Hoosier* means.[1] Or they laughed at Kentucky, for having a statewide total of twenty-three teeth.

But today all of these states are laughing at Florida. *Everybody* is laughing at Florida. *Mississippi* is laughing at Florida.

How did this happen? As far as I have been able to determine without doing any research, the turning point was the presidential election of 2000. You remember. It was Al Gore against George Bush. On Election Night almost all of the other states were able to figure out pretty quickly who they voted for. But not Florida. Florida had no earthly idea who it had voted for. At first, it looked like maybe Gore had won the state, but then it looked like Bush had, but then suddenly it was Al again, and then it was Bush again. At one point, William Shatner appeared to be in contention. It was insane. By dawn we still had no winner, and network TV political analysts were openly shooting heroin on camera.

---

1. Some historians believe it comes from the Shawnee expression "ho'o-sa'ars," or "people who cannot explain their nickname."

Meanwhile, the morning skies over the state were darkened by vast fleets of transport planes swooping in from Washington, D.C., opening their doors and dropping tens of thousands of election lawyers. Some landed in the Everglades and were consumed by Burmese pythons. But, tragically, many survived, and, without taking time to remove their parachutes, they commenced filing lawsuits.

This was the beginning of more than a month of intensive 24/7 TV news coverage of the Florida elections. This coverage did not present a positive image of Florida. It featured endlessly replayed videos of deeply confused Florida election officials squinting at Florida ballots that were apparently designed by dyslexic lemurs and then turned over to deeply confused Florida voters, many of whom apparently voted for nobody for president, or voted for two presidents, or used the ballots to dislodge pieces of brisket from between their teeth. Some voters apparently just drooled on their ballots, not that this stopped battalions of Washington lawyers from passionately debating which candidate these voters were drooling *for*.

This gruesomely unflattering coverage of Florida ran nonstop, day after hellish day. It finally ended when the U.S. Supreme Court ruled, in a 7–2 decision, that Florida should be given back to Spain.

OK, not really. But by then that was basically how the rest

of the nation felt. And the nation did not forget. The nation had formed a negative, stereotyped image of Florida as being a subtropical festival of stupid. From then on, every time anything stupid happened here, America rolled its national eyeballs and went, "There goes Florida again!"

Journalists have built entire careers on chronicling Florida people doing stupid things. Somebody started a popular Twitter account called Florida Man, which consists entirely of links to news items about Florida men doing stupid things: *Florida Man Seen Firing Musket at Cars While Dressed as Pirate*; *Florida Man Poses as Superman on Side of Road While Pantless, Urinating*; *Florida Man Sets Home on Fire with Bomb Made from Bowling Ball*; *Florida Man Seen Trying to Sell Live Shark in Grocery Store Parking Lot*; *Florida Man Slashes 88-Year-Old Woman's Tires with Ice Pick for Sitting in His Favorite Bingo Seat*; *Knife-wielding Florida Man Tries to Rescue Imaginary Girlfriend from Garbage Truck*; *Florida Man Says He Danced on Patrol Car in Order to Escape Vampires*; *Florida Man Proudly Claims He's the First Man Ever to Vape Semen*; *Florida Man Seen Masturbating into Stuffed Animal in Walmart Bedding Department*; *Florida Man Shoots Sister in Butt with BB Gun Because She Gave Him Penis-shaped Birthday Cake*; and on and on and on.

To judge from the news, there is no end to the stupid

activities that Florida men, and women, engage in. Quite often—probably because of Florida's moderate climate—they choose to engage in these activities naked. In some other state, a person might say to himself, "I believe I shall pose as Superman by the side of the road!" But in Florida, that person is also going to say, "But first, I shall remove my pants!"

Why do there seem to be so many stupid people in Florida? Is there a scientific explanation?

Yes, there is.

## A Scientific Explanation
## For Why There Are So Many
## Stupid People in Florida
## And Why This Is Not Really Florida's Fault

Imagine several hundred laboratory rats that have been selected at random from the general rat population, so they vary in size, strength, color, intelligence, flea count, etc.

Now imagine that laboratory scientists scientifically place these rats in the center of a large box that is open on top but has high walls around the perimeter. The box is shaped roughly like a rectangle, but at the lower right corner there is a long, skinny dead-end corridor jutting out.

The rats are able to roam freely inside the box. Almost all of them, sooner or later, venture down the skinny corridor. After checking it out, they decide to leave. The intelligent ones immediately realize they need to turn around and go back out the way they came in. The ones with average intelligence, or even slightly below-average intelligence, take longer, but eventually they, too, figure it out. But what happens to the really stupid rats?

That's right: *They elect the governor of Illinois.*

No, seriously, because these rats aren't smart enough to turn around and retrace their steps, they become stuck down there in the corridor, wandering cluelessly this way and that, unable to figure out how to get out.

This is exactly what has happened in Florida, except instead of rats we have people, and instead of walls we have the Atlantic Ocean and the Gulf of Mexico. People come down here all the time. Most of them, sooner or later, decide to leave, but the stupid ones can't figure out how to do this. So they remain, and in time are issued ballots.

The point—and remember that this is not just my opinion, this is a *fact*, based on an actual laboratory experiment conducted by imaginary scientists—is that, yes, Florida, because of its unique shape and warm climate, does have an unusually high percentage of low IQ people doing stupid things, frequently naked. But most of these people *came here from other states*, the very same states that are laughing at Florida. Those of us who live here have to contend with not just our native-born stupid but *your* stupid, too. We are like Ellis Island, except instead of taking the huddled masses yearning to breathe free, we take people who yearn to pleasure themselves into a stuffed animal at Walmart.

But it's not just the Stupid Factor that has given Florida its unfortunate national reputation. There is also the Weirdness Factor. Things keep *happening* in Florida—things that are similar to things that happen in other states except that there is some mutant element, some surreal twist, that makes the rest of the nation nod its national head and think, "Ah… Florida." Here's a news headline from 2015:

---

## VANILLA ICE ARRESTED FOR STEALING POOL HEATER FROM A FORECLOSED HOME

---

This headline does not mention Florida. But you know that everyone reading it immediately assumed, correctly, that the incident occurred in Florida, because while you might imagine a pool heater being stolen in some other state, you cannot imagine another state where the heater would allegedly be stolen by *Vanilla Ice*.[2] That is what I mean by the Florida Weirdness Factor.

Here's another 2015 example: A tractor-trailer blew a tire on Interstate 95 and went off the road into some woods in Volusia County, Florida. The crash resulted in a fatality.

"Wait a minute," I hear you saying. "That's unfortunate, but it's not *weird*. Accidents involving fatalities happen all the time."

Yes, but in this case, the fatality was a *shark*. The tractor-trailer was carrying four sharks from the Florida Keys to an aquarium in Coney Island in New York City and one of the sharks was ejected during the crash. Fortunately, it didn't hit anybody, but the fact remains that there was, briefly, an airborne shark on Interstate 95, and it could have hit a car, which would have been tragic, by which I mean pretty funny.

The point is, Florida is the only state I am aware of where

---

2. Mr. Ice avoided grand theft charges by agreeing to pay a fine and do community service. He said it was all a "misunderstanding," and I, for one, believe him. Who among us has never mistakenly taken a pool heater? Many's the time I have emptied my pockets and said, "Where the heck did THAT come from?"

a shark was killed in a traffic accident.[3] Speaking of which: Florida is also the only state I am aware of in which a woman crashed her car because she was shaving her privates. According to the *Key West Citizen*, this woman was heading for Key West on the Overseas Highway. Technically, she should not have been driving, since her license had been revoked, but let's not nitpick. She was going to visit her boyfriend, and—in the words of the state trooper who later arrested her—she "wanted to be ready for the visit." So she decided to shave what is known in medical terminology as her Bikini Area.

How do you think she elected to do this? Do you think she pulled over to the side of the road and stopped the vehicle? Of course not! That would have wasted valuable time. Instead, she had the person sitting in the passenger seat—who happened to be her ex-husband—steer the car while she shaved. The fact that her ex-husband was in the car is a textbook example of the Florida Weirdness Factor.

So they were motoring along at 45 miles per hour, the ex-husband steering and the woman operating the accelerator

---

3. It's also the state where two men attempted to transport a live shark on Miami's downtown People Mover during rush hour, but I covered that in another book.

whilst tending to her Area. What could possibly go wrong, right? Unfortunately, the car in front of them—in a one-in-a-million fluke occurrence that nobody could have foreseen—slowed down to make a turn, and Team Steering/Shaving slammed into it.

The *Key West Citizen* quoted the state trooper as saying: "'If I wasn't there, I wouldn't have believed it. About 10 years ago I stopped a guy in the exact same spot... who had three or four syringes sticking out of his arm. It was just surreal and I thought, "Nothing will ever beat this." Well, this takes it.'"

By the way: The driving-while-shaving woman hailed from Indiana. That's right: *She was a Hoosier.*

One more Florida motoring story: In March of 2015, a Tampa resident named Robert Abercrombie pulled his eight-year-old son's loose tooth. How is this a motoring story? It is a motoring story because Abercrombie pulled the tooth *with his Chevrolet Camaro.* Yes. He tied one end of a string to the tooth and the other end to the back of the Camaro. Then, with his son standing in the street behind the car, he revs the engine and roars off, yanking the tooth out as clean as a whistle, if a whistle had gums that could bleed. This might conceivably happen in some other state, but the wrinkle that makes this a true Florida Weird story is that Abercrombie is a professional wrestler.

**Fact:** More professional wrestlers reside in Florida than in any other state.[4]

Abercrombie wrestles under the professional moniker "Rob Venomous." On his Facebook page, under "Personal Interests," Mr. Venomous lists "Meeting new people . . . beating up new people." There is only one state where this man would reside and practice amateur dentistry.

Of course, not every Florida Weirdness story has a feel-good storybook ending involving a clearly relieved eight-year-old with bleeding gums watching his tooth bounce gaily down the street behind a Camaro. There are plenty of Florida tragedies and we should not make light of them, although we cannot help but observe how truly weird they are.

One vivid example of a Florida tragedy that got national attention because of the weird factor involved the death in 2012 of a man at a Deerfield Beach reptile store. There are many reptile stores in Florida, especially South Florida. I don't recall ever seeing a reptile store when I lived in the Northeast, but down here they're everywhere, like Starbucks,

---

4. I totally made this fact up, but I bet it's true.

except instead of lattes they sell snakes. If you're the kind of person who frequently remarks, "I wish to purchase a reptile but I don't wish to travel a long distance," then this is definitely the state for you.

But getting back to our tragic yet weird story: Try to guess what would cause this man to die at a reptile store. If you guessed that he was bitten by a venomous snake, thank you for playing, but no. The cause of his death—and here we are definitely in Florida-only territory—was *eating cockroaches*. The store held a cockroach-eating contest; before that, there was a worm-eating contest, which this man also entered.

Now try to guess *why* this man entered a cockroach-eating contest. To pay the mortgage? To defray urgent medical expenses? Please do not be silly. He was trying to *win a snake*. Yes. First prize was a ball python—which, for the record, the man did not even intend to keep for his personal use. He planned to give it to a friend. Anyway, he won the contest, but tragically the cockroaches did not agree with him. The reptile store stated, on Facebook, that the snake "now belongs to his estate." So there's that.

I think we can agree that this would not have happened in a normal state.

So to summarize:

- Florida, as a result of being a peninsula, through no fault of its own, contains an unusually high percentage of stupid people, many from other states such as (not to single out any one state) Indiana.
- Florida also—again, through no fault of its own, and possibly as a result of some kind of powerful Weirdness Ray being beamed at us from a distant planet inhabited by an advanced alien civilization that enjoys playing interstellar pranks—has a random Weirdness Factor that blankets the state like a fog, seeping into what should be everyday events and causing them to mutate into events involving airborne sharks or Vanilla Ice.

And so we are The Joke State, the state everybody loves to mock. Even people who have moved to Florida from other states continue to mock it. South Florida is infested by former New Yorkers who never get tired of pointing out—in that quiet, understated New Yorker voice that can penetrate concrete at six hundred yards—how pathetic Florida is, because we're a bunch of yokels down here and we don't know how to make decent pizza or bagels and we're terrible sports fans and our restaurants suck and our newspapers are a joke because they're not *The New York Times* and our theater is pathetic compared to Broadway and we don't have real museums and it bears repeating that the pizza and bagels down here are *terrible* and our water tastes funny and there are too many insects and blah-blah-blah the pizza blah-blah-blah the bagels blah-blah-bl—

## SHUT UP, NEW YORKERS.

I apologize for using an all-caps bolded font but it gets really tiresome listening to these people who have chosen, voluntarily, of their own free will, to leave the paradise of New York and move to Florida, and who apparently have no intention of going back, but who *cannot stop* declaring how vastly superior New York is. I myself grew up in the New York suburbs and lived in the city for a couple of years. I still go there often, and, when I do, I enjoy its many positive qualities. I don't dwell on the negatives. I don't, for example, observe that during warm weather much of Manhattan smells like vomit-soaked garbage being boiled in a large vat of urine. I don't complain about the traffic, or the prices, or the people behind you on the sidewalk who become annoyed if you delay them by walking slower than 23 miles per hour. Nor do I observe that when you eat in popular restaurants—after

17

waiting an hour or more to be seated, of course—the tables are jammed so close together that adjoining diners sometimes accidentally put their food into your mouth.

I'm willing to overlook New York's flaws because I believe every place has flaws. But these days nobody overlooks Florida's flaws. Nobody cuts Florida any slack. Florida is everybody's punching bag. I am looking at an Internet site called Thrillist, which is one of those sites with content generated by hip, smart young writers who years ago might have practiced actual journalism but who in the modern media world are reduced to writing clickbait lists with headlines like "Fourteen Kinds of Worms That Are Probably in Your Body Right Now." The particular list I'm looking at is titled "THE DEFINITIVE AND FINAL RANKING OF ALL 50 STATES." It begins with the state ranked fiftieth, dead last. Of course it's Florida. Here, in its entirety, is the "explanation" given by the writers for this ranking:

> *When putting together a list such as this, there can be some temptation to defy popular expectations, and go against the grain. However, Florida's awfulness resume is so staggeringly impressive that it couldn't go any other way. You were born for this. Embrace it.*

Notice that the Thrillist writers felt no need to offer a single actual specific reason *why* Florida is the worst state. It just is, and everybody knows why, and we Floridians, in the view of Thrillist, should just shut up and "embrace it."

Here, according to Thrillist, are the four best states (seriously):

1. Michigan.
2. Maine.
3. Kentucky.
4. Wisconsin.

Now, I could note a couple of obvious things about these states. I could note that the largest city in Michigan is Detroit, where the value of the average single-family home has declined to approximately the price of a Happy Meal. Or I could note that the weather in Michigan, Maine and Wisconsin during winter—defined as September through late June—is pretty much the same as the climate on the lunar surface. I could also note that Kentucky is, with all due respect, Kentucky.

But I will not mention these things. Instead, I will go to Google and see if I can find out (a) whether people are moving away from these four wonderful top-ranked states, and (b) if so, where they are moving to.

Hey, guess what? It turns out that a lot of people ARE moving out of Michigan, Maine, Kentucky and Wisconsin. Apparently, these people do not base their life decisions on Thrillist. And here is an even MORE amazing fact: The Number One destination of people moving out of *all four of these states* is—you guessed it—Indiana.

No, seriously, it's Florida. Florida is also the number one destination of people leaving a number of other states, including both New York and New Jersey, thousands and thousands of them every year, somehow tearing themselves away from the indescribable magnificence of the pizza, and, of course, the bagels—we can't forget the bagels!—to move to Florida. In fact, people from all over are moving to Florida. Florida's population is growing like crazy. It's now bigger than New York's. Embrace *that*, Thrillist writers.

So we have an apparent contradiction:

On the one hand, the national consensus is that Florida is a stupid weird insane dysfunctional hellhole that is also—I forgot to mention this earlier—a hurricane zone that is soon going to be largely submerged when global climate change causes the seas to rise to the point where vast herds of lobsters roam what is now Interstate 95.

On the other hand, *people keep coming here.* And most of them—even the non-stupid ones—decide to stay here.

The question is: Why?

To answer that question properly, we need to do some research. Specifically, we need to conduct an objective, in-depth study of the Florida immigration phenomenon—a study involving a professionally designed and conducted survey of a scientifically selected sample of immigrants to the state over a significant time period, and a thorough statistical analysis of the results. I think we can all agree that such an effort would be unbelievably boring. I nearly nodded off just typing about it. So instead I'll just tell you some of the reasons why I, personally, like living in Florida:

## The weather is warm.

Almost any day of the year I could walk out my front door naked and be perfectly physically comfortable until the police tasered me. Granted, sometimes in the summer (defined as June through the following June) it gets a little too warm down here, but too warm beats the hell out of too cold. Too cold means if you stay outside too long, you will die. Too warm means you might have to have another beer.

Since I moved here, I have never, not once, had to scrape ice off my car. Yes, I often scrape off deceased flying insects the size of LeBron James, and once I scraped off an ex-toad.

But never ice or snow. One of the great joys of Florida life is watching CNN on a weekday morning in January when the top story is BLIZZARD BLANKETS NORTHEAST and there's video of miserable commuters whose ice-covered cars are sliding sideways into ice-covered cars driven by other miserable commuters, all of them doomed to days and weeks and months more misery in a hideous frozen wasteland where the highlight of the average working day is getting all the way across the Dunkin' Donuts parking lot without being attacked by wolves.

We *love* watching that, down here in Florida. Sometimes we get so emotional watching it, even at 7 a.m., that we have to have ourselves a cold beer.

## The taxes are low.

Florida's taxes are close to the lowest in the nation. There is no personal income tax. And yet our state government is excellent.

No, that's a lie. Our state government is incompetent and corrupt. But before we rush to any judgments, let's examine this chart comparing Florida with some other randomly selected states:

| State | Level of Taxation | Type of Government |
|---|---|---|
| Florida | Low | Incompetent and Corrupt |
| California | High | Incompetent and Corrupt |
| Illinois | High | Incompetent and Corrupt |
| New Jersey | High | Incompetent and Corrupt |
| New York | High | Incompetent and Corrupt |

This chart tells us that the residents of California, Illinois, New Jersey and New York—not to mention other states—are paying unnecessarily high taxes for the quality of state government they're getting. These people could move to Florida and get corrupt and incompetent government for *much* less. "More Value for Your Dollar" should be the official state motto of Florida, except that the Florida government would spell it "More Value for You're Dollar" and nobody would notice the mistake until after all the stationery was printed.

## The women are amazing.

I am not saying that women in other states are not attractive. Nor am I saying that attractiveness is the only quality that matters in a woman. Nor am I saying that there should even be such a concept as "attractiveness," because women are not objects to be objectified as if they were some kind of objects or something. Nor am I saying, as a member of the white male patriarchy, that I am not, by definition, oppressive misogynistic vermin scum who should receive extensive mandatory training in gender sensitivity followed by castration with poorly maintained power tools. What I *am* saying is that if you *were* the kind of unenlightened male who enjoyed looking at attractive women—which would, of course, be wrong—then you would look at the women of Florida and say to yourself, quote, "Whoa."

This is especially true of women in Miami. They really make an effort. Let's say it's Saturday morning and a woman decides to go to the supermarket. A woman in some other part of the country—I am looking at you, The Midwest— might decide that, hey, it's just the supermarket, no need to get all gussied-up. So she puts on comfortable jeans, comfortable sneakers and a comfortable, loose-fitting T-shirt, usually with something written on it such as R.E.O. SPEED-WAGON 1995 SEVEN STATE WORLD TOUR. This also happens to be exactly the outfit her husband[5] would wear to the su-

---

5. Assuming she is married. To a man. Which, of course, *she does not have to be.*

permarket. Sometimes they accidentally put on each other's clothes.

Not Miami Woman. She would not wipe up cat vomit with a loose-fitting T-shirt, let alone wear one in public. Miami Woman does not own loose-fitting *anything*. If she ever went camping in the wilderness—which she would not, because the wilderness lacks nail salons—she would sleep in a form-fitting sleeping bag inside a form-fitting *tent*.

Miami Woman keeps herself in shape and spends a lot of time on her appearance, and she frankly thinks she looks pretty damn good, and most of the time she is correct. When she goes out in public—defined as "beyond the immediate bathroom"—she makes sure she is totally put together. The result is that Miami—in fact, South Florida in general—is swarming with what a less evolved person than myself would call smoking hot babes.

A few years ago a guy I know was visiting from another state, and he accompanied me to the supermarket. There were many women there, but I was not particularly distracted, because (a) I am used to it, and (b) none of these women measured up to my wife, who is extremely attractive and will eventually read this. But my friend was not used to it. He was walking into freezer cases. His eyeballs were falling out of their sockets and rolling around the produce section.

"Is it *always* like this?" he asked me.

"Pretty much," I said.

"If I lived here," he said, "I would go to the supermarket *constantly*. I would buy my groceries *one grape at a time*."

And that's just the supermarket. You should see how good Miami Woman looks at the *beach*.

Q: How good does she look?

A: Frequently the tide, after coming in, refuses to go back out.

Now, don't get me wrong. I'm not saying the United States is some kind of giant beauty pageant. We can't rank a state based on some superficial quality such as the physical beauty of its women; it's important to consider other factors, such as the warmth of the state's climate and the lowness of its taxes. All I'm saying is that if the United States *were* a giant beauty pageant, Florida, based on Miami alone, would kick your state's ass.

Also I am told that the men of Florida are exceptionally good-looking. I cannot confirm this, because I don't pay much attention to them. My wife assures me that she doesn't either.

## It's not boring.

Florida is one of the least boring places on the planet. As we have established, things keep *happening* here. Granted, many of these things are bizarre or stupid or dangerous. Often drugs are involved. Or alligators. We cannot rule out the possibility of alligators on drugs. We cannot rule *anything* out, because we never know what will happen next in Florida. We know only that, any minute now, *something will*. That's what makes Florida more interesting than states such as, no offense, Nebraska.

Don't get me wrong: Nebraska is a fine state, with a proud tradition of vegetables growing there. Its very nickname is The Cornhusker State, reflecting the fact that it contains a huge quantity of corn, which Nebraskans apparently take pride in husking. But this is not necessarily a compelling reason to go there. "Let's go to Nebraska and watch corn being husked!" is something you rarely hear people say when they are looking for excitement. They are far more likely to say, "Let's go to that parade in Key West where the marchers wear basically just paint."

Now, before you Cornhuskers complain that I am being unfair, yes, I know there is more to Nebraska than just corn.

There is also a huge quantity of soybeans. There are even some tourist attractions. According to the official Nebraska website, one of the state's top attractions is a geological formation called Chimney Rock, which, as its name suggests, is a rock. Here's what the website says (really) about Chimney Rock:

> *According to early fur traders, Native Americans named the rock Elk Penis after the penis of the adult male elk.[6] This made more sense to those who had lived for centuries on the plains than comparing the rock to a feature from a white man's building. Prim and proper usage among Anglo-Americans, though, overwhelmingly preferred the more delicate name chimney.*

Far be it from me to offer unsolicited advice, but if I were in charge of Nebraska tourism, I would definitely change the official name of Chimney Rock back to Elk Penis. I bet tourists would swarm to the state, if only to buy the T-shirt. Then, while they were in Nebraska, they would become exposed to the state's many other attractions. ("Look, kids! *More* corn!")

---

6. As opposed to the penis of the adult female elk.

But I digress. My point is that Florida is not boring. Although if you *want* boring, Florida has that, too. For example, we have the Everglades. Biologists will tell you that the Everglades is one of the Earth's most interesting ecosystems. What they will not tell you is that the word *ecosystem* comes from the ancient Greek words *ecosys*, which means "really," and *tem*, which means "boring swamp that reeks of frog doody." So anytime Florida gets too exciting for you, you can just wade out into the Everglades and stand around up to your thighs in muck and swat mosquitoes until you have calmed down sufficiently. At which point you will be eaten by a python.

Florida: Even our boring parts are exciting.

At this point you are saying: "Dave, you have convinced me that Florida is superior to other states in the areas of climate, taxation, hotness of women and not being boring. But what about other areas, such as education, health care, employment, housing, environmental sustainability and infrastructure? Does Florida perform well in these areas?"

OK, not necessarily. But who cares, because:

*Florida has Disney World.*

Think about what this means. Never mind, I will tell you:

It means that wherever you live in Florida, you have easy access to *the number one family theme resort in the world.* My family can get into our car in Miami and, in just three and a half hours, we can be in the Magic Kingdom, standing in a four-hour line to get into Space Mountain. You cannot put a price tag on a family theme experience like that.

I could go on and on, listing all the good things about Florida. I could point out that it is the only state where you can get a really good *mojito.* Or that it's the nation's flattest state, so if you fall down after a few *mojitos,* you will not roll far. Or that Florida is a very tolerant state, willing to grant a driver's license to pretty much any organism consisting of more than one cell. Or that Florida leads the nation in lightning strikes, which is pretty cool as long as the lightning does not strike you personally.

But I think I have more than proved my point. Florida, despite what you hear from the haters in the cold boring high-tax Elk-Penis-attraction states with (no offense) ugly women, is a great state. This book is a celebration of that greatness—starting with Florida's past, which is filled with fascinating historic events that I intend to find out about soon on Wikipedia, and moving forward to the present, which—believe it or not—is happening right now. Come with me, then, and let us together explore the many wonders of

The Sunshine State, from Key West, way down at the very bottom, to whatever wonder is at the very top, and everything in between, except the parts we leave out. When we're done, I think you will truly understand the feelings of the great Spanish explorer Juan Tostones de Bodega, who, upon setting foot in Florida for the first time in the year 1503, is said to have observed: *"Esa araña tiene el tamaño de un guante de receptor."*[7] He died only hours later, but his words are as true today as they ever were.

7. "That spider is the size of a catcher's mitt."

# A BRIEF HISTORY OF FLORIDA

For millions of years, Florida was uninhabited, because it was geographically remote, not to mention several hundred feet beneath the surface of the Atlantic, which meant insurance rates were very high. Gradually, however, Global Rising caused Florida to emerge from the ocean, and today the state is above sea level except during certain months.

The first humans arrived in Florida twenty thousand years ago, having crossed the land bridge from Asia and made the arduous trek across North America in search of Spring Break. These early inhabitants left primitive archaeological artifacts that can still be seen today, including the world's oldest-known stone bong.

In time, the population of Florida started to grow—probably, scientists now believe, as a result of people having sex with each other. Eventually, these indigenous peoples spread out across Florida and formed Native American tribes, including the Tequestas, Mohicans, Cheyennes, Seminoles, Gators, Presbyterians and Kansas City Chiefs. These tribes established thriving, sophisticated societies based on hitting things with rocks until they became edible. Sometimes the tribes would fight wars, but after maybe fifteen minutes they would stop because of the humidity.

Thus Florida was a prosperous and peaceful place until the early sixteenth century when the first Europeans arrived in the form of Spanish explorers who had been lured by the legend of the *Pájaro Temprano*, which told of a mythical place where, if you were seated before 4:30 p.m., you got a steeply discounted entrée. The Spaniards named the new land *La Pascua de la Florida* (literally, "The Sunshine State") and claimed it for Spain, seeing as how there was nobody there except for several hundred thousand natives.

In 1763, Spain and England decided to end the Seven Years' War because it started in 1756 and they couldn't agree on a new name for it. In the peace settlement, Spain gave Florida to England as part of a package that also included 167 trillion mosquitoes. England, seeking to link Florida with its colonies to the north, erected a two-hundred-mile-long line of orange highway-construction barrels, which can still be seen today.

For the next two decades, English settlers attempted to engage in agriculture, which mainly consisted of fending off alligators with hoes.[1] Finally in 1783, England said the hell with it and gave Florida back to Spain, reserving the right for English citizens to return on holiday and lie on the beach until their skin was the color of Hawaiian Punch.

Meanwhile, to the north, the United States was forming. The Spanish authorities tried to keep the Americans out of Florida, but settlers from Georgia kept coming across the border and erecting primitive log Waffle Houses. Eventually, Spain gave up and tried to give Florida back to England, which, of course, refused, as did France, Germany, Poland, Switzerland, Australia, Egypt, Japan and the Republic of Fiji. Finally, in 1821, Florida became an American territory, which it remains to this day in many areas.

---

1. To clarify: The *settlers* had the hoes. The alligators had machetes.

At first there were land disputes between the U.S. government and the Native American tribes, but these were eventually settled via a treaty under which the government got the land and the tribes got to leave. In 1845, Florida became the twenty-seventh state in the union, choosing Tallahassee as its capital, which got a good laugh from the other states because Tallahassee is located in Alabama.

In those days, the Florida economy was strictly agricultural, with the main crop being cotton, which was grown on large plantations and gathered into bales, which were then transported to seaports, where they were thrown away because of mildew. This was hard work, but much of the labor was provided by slaves, who were always willing to lend a helping hand in exchange for not being beaten to death.

In 1865, the Civil War broke out, although Florida did not find out about it until 1883, when it was too late to really get involved. Meanwhile, the state's farmers had given up on cotton and were growing oranges, which were popular in the Northern states. One fateful day, a Florida farmer decided, as a prank, to ship up some grapefruit. At the time, nobody in Florida considered grapefruit to be edible; it was used exclusively as a weapon. But, incredibly, Northerners actually *ate* it, apparently believing that anything tasting that bad must be healthy. This marketing breakthrough paved the way for such "health foods" as tofu, which is actually a waste by-product of the manufacture of linoleum, and quinoa, which gets its name from the Bolivian word for "gravel."

January 1, 1900, marked the dawn of the twentieth century, although because of a broken telegraph wire Florida did not find out about this until July 18, 1903. For the next decade or so, the state remained fairly isolated, although it played a pivotal role in World War I on November 10, 1918, when American biplanes—in an action that was widely condemned by international human-rights organizations—dropped several dozen grapefruit on Germany, which surrendered immediately.

World War I was followed by the Roaring Twenties, a time when Americans went to speakeasies, where they drank bathtub gin[2] until they were so impaired that they believed it would be a sound financial strategy to invest, sight unseen, in real estate located at or below sea level in a tropical cyclone zone. This resulted in the first Florida Land Boom, during which Miami went from being a sleepy village to a thriving metropolis, until the Hurricane of 1926 turned it back into a sleepy village, but with a lot more kindling.

---

2. Probably laced with grapefruit juice.

This was followed by the Great Depression, which was very bad in Florida.

Q: How bad was it?

A: Some families resorted to eating grapefruit.

The only ray of economic hope during the thirties was the growth of Florida's tourism industry, which was boosted by the construction of such "only in Florida" attractions as Alligator World, Alligator Land, Alligator Swamp, Alligator Jungle, Alligator Jamboree, Alligator Rodeo, Alligato-Rama and Alligators Out the Wazoo. These attractions consisted of alligators—some of which were clearly deceased—lying motionless in odiferous muck for days at a time. But tourists flocked to them anyway, because back then people were a lot stupider than they are today. (This also explains the popularity of the yo-yo.)

The next major event was World War II, during which Florida, once it found out what was going on, was totally on the American side.

In 1956, the federal government began work on the Interstate Highway System, an ambitious project intended to realize the dream that someday, thanks to a vast network of safe, well-engineered, high-speed roads, Americans in formerly isolated communities would be able to get into their cars and, within a matter of hours, stop at a random exit to pee. Before long, millions of Americans were using the Interstate system to reach Florida, where—thanks to the modern miracle of air-conditioning—they were able to remain indoors until it was time to go home.

Florida also got a big economic boost when the federal government decided to locate the space program in Cape Canaveral, which was an ideal location for launching rockets because over the centuries hurricanes had blown away most of the gravity.[3]

In the sixties, Florida's population grew rapidly as large numbers of retirees moved down from the north, seeking an affordable place to grow lengthy nose hairs and drive 14 miles an hour in the left lane. At the same time waves of Cuban refugees, fleeing the Castro regime, settled in the Miami area and, like so many immigrants before them, set about creating their own foreign policy. Also during the sixties, millions of college students flocked to Florida's beach towns each spring to engage in youthful hijinks and pass out in puddles of vomit.

Meanwhile, Walt Disney was buying up huge tracts of

---

3. **Fact:** In Cape Canaveral, coconuts fall *up*.

land near the sleepy[4] Central Florida town of Orlando, but nobody figured out what he was up to because he used the secret code name "Balt Bisney." Disney World opened on October 1, 1971, drawing 400,000 visitors, many of whom are still trying to remember where they parked. Central Florida soon became a major tourism destination boasting many theme attractions, including Movie Galaxy Universe Planet, Wet 'n' Damp, Licensed Merchandise Land, and World of Sea Creatures Delighted to Be Trapped in Tanks Swimming Around and Around and Around for the Rest of Their Lives. Otherwise, nothing much happened in the seventies, unless you count disco, which sucked as much in Florida as it did everywhere else.

During the seventies and eighties, Florida grew rapidly and prospered because it had a good climate, low taxes and an energetic economy based on tourism and guys importing narcotics by the ton. Also, ammunition sales were very strong.

In the nineties, Florida experienced many important historical events that we are unable to tell you about because for some reason the Wikipedia article stops before then.

---

4. We are using "sleepy" in the sense of "not too bright."

Today, Florida—once a quiet backwater—is a modern and dynamic state that has totally entered the twenty-first century, except during presidential elections, when it reverts to 437 B.C. It is a truly exceptional place, as we can see from these:

### FACTS ABOUT FLORIDA TODAY

- Florida is the third most-populous state.
- It is actually in second place if you count dead people.
- More than 1,000 people move to Florida every day.
- Roughly eight of these people understand the purpose of the turn signal.
- Florida's government is divided into three branches: the executive, the judicial and the criminal.
- Under Florida's "stand your ground" law, it is legal to shoot anybody for any reason as long as you are standing on the ground.
- Although the state supreme court recently ruled that "sitting is also OK."
- Currently, the number one industry in Florida is attorneys on billboards asking if you have been in an accident, followed by tourism, reptile sales and buttocks enhancement.

- Florida is the world's largest cruise-passenger market, with an average pre-buffet weight of 357 pounds per passenger.
- Florida is home to both the Shuffleboard Hall of Fame *and* Carrot Top.[5]
- Also supposedly there are some museums.
- For years the highest point in Florida was LeBron James, but then he moved back to Cleveland.
- *Cleveland*, for God's sake.
- Florida has two separate rivers named Withlacoochee, which sounds like a slang term for a sexually transmitted disease.
- Florida also has a river named Pithlachascotee. It is sometimes called the Cootie, for short. We don't know why, and we don't *want* to know why.
- Here are some other actual names of Florida rivers: Alapahoochee, Caloosahatchee, Econlockhatchee, Fakahatchee, Ichetucknee and Hontoon Dead.
- Fort Lauderdale is sometimes called The Venice of America by people who clearly have never been to Venice.
- In Florida, cockroaches are called Palmetto bugs,

---

5. This fact is actually true.

because if they hear you call them cockroaches, they will become enraged and destroy your kitchen.

- Natives of the Florida Keys often refer to themselves as Conchs,[6] and for good reason: They have been drinking.
- In 2015, the official state tourism marketing corporation, Visit Florida, named as a "Florida ambassador," in which capacity he will represent the state: Pitbull.
- Seriously.
- Mr. Bull, a professional "rap" artist, has authored numerous tunes about having sex,[7] doing drugs, shooting people, selling drugs, having sex on drugs, shooting people over drugs, etc.
- In other words, he is perfect.

6. Pronounced "Conchs."

7. One of his tunes is titled "Everybody Fucks."

# THE
# SKUNK APE

I set out from Miami driving west on Route 41, the Tamiami Trail, which connects Miami on the east coast of Florida with Tampa on the west. At the Miami end, it's also known as *Calle Ocho*—"Eighth Street"—which is considered the heart of Little Havana, the place where the TV news crews go to shoot man-in-the-street video of authentic Cubans drinking authentic Cuban coffee and reacting to whatever is happening in Cuba. You can spend a day here and never hear any language but Spanish.

I head west on the Trail to Krome Avenue, which is just a few miles from Calle Ocho in linear space but light-years away in ambience. Across Krome, the world changes, quite suddenly, from city to swamp. This is the edge of the Everglades, Miami's vast, wild, weird backyard.

For many decades, most people—most white people, anyway—viewed the Everglades as a waste of space, a bug-infested bog to be drained and turned into something useful. We now know, of course, that the Everglades are a unique, precious, fragile and irreplaceable wetlands ecosystem. But I'll be honest: This place has always kind of creeped me out. Strange things live out here; strange things happen out here.

For example: On the northwest corner of the Krome Avenue intersection, just inside the swamp, is a three-hundred-room hotel/casino resort operated by the Miccosukee Indian Tribe. One day in 2007, police received a report that two men were breaking into cars in the parking lot. Police responded and caught one of the men. The other ran away and dove into a nearby pond. That was a poor decision: This particular pond happened to be the residence of a large alligator, known to the resort staff as "Poncho." The next day divers recovered what was left of the man fifty feet underwater.

I know some pretty crazy things have happened in Las Vegas, but I doubt that anybody on a Vegas casino property was ever eaten by an alligator.

Poncho is not alone: There are a couple of hundred thousand gators in the Everglades, and maybe a billion bullfrogs. There are also panthers out there, and bears, all kinds of birds, and God knows how many snakes, including Burmese pythons just about long enough to be used, if you could straighten them out, for first-down measurements.

And there's exotic human wildlife in the Everglades. There are poachers out there, and smugglers, and other well-armed people who seriously—I mean, *seriously*—value their privacy. There are fugitives hiding for one reason or another, lying low in a place where it's famously easy to disappear. There have been hidden commando bases out there where, for decades, various paramilitary groups—some known to the U.S. government, some not—trained for secret missions. There are stories of Indian burial sites where the ground is littered with artifacts worth a fortune, just lying around for the taking, if you could find them, which you can't.

This is an inadequate list of the elements that make the Everglades weird. It's safe to say that there are many more strange things going on out there that very few people know about, or ever will.

So, what with the combination of wildlife and weirdness, I have never viewed the Everglades as a place where I want to hang out. I have viewed it as a big flat space to be driven across as quickly as possible, much like Nebraska, but with a funkier aroma. When I'm crossing the 'glades, I crank up the car radio and zip along at 70, 80, 90 miles an hour, my only interaction with the unique, precious, fragile and irreplaceable wetlands ecosystem around me coming in the form of flying insects the size of cocker spaniels splatting on my windshield.

But today I'm going to stop in the Everglades. Because today I'm on the trail of what could be the strangest of all the strange things out there, the weirdest of the weird: the skunk ape.

The skunk ape is Florida's version of Bigfoot. It is said to walk erect, like a man, but its body is completely covered with hair like an ape, or the cast of *Duck Dynasty*. It allegedly stands seven feet tall and reeks of an odor like rotten eggs or worse. It is said to like lima beans.

Over the decades, many people claim to have seen the skunk ape, or its footprints. There are a few photos, and even a video, but as is so often the case with this kind of thing, the images are blurry or inconclusive.

Dozens of journalists and TV shows—including Comedy Central, which sent Stephen Colbert to the Everglades—have done stories on the skunk ape. *Smithsonian* magazine, among others, ran a long investigative piece about it. Some serious mainstream researchers have also looked into the sightings. But so far, nobody has found any conclusive proof—

at least, not the kind accepted by scientists—that the skunk ape exists. The consensus in the scientific community is that either people are seeing some other animal—maybe a bear, maybe somebody's pet orangutan that escaped into the wild—or the skunk ape is a hoax, some guy running around in a gorilla suit. But as I say, plenty of people claim they've seen it, and plenty more believe it's real.

If you read the skunk ape stories, one name comes up again and again over the years: Dave Shealy. He claims to have seen the skunk ape three times. He shot the best-known skunk ape video, which shows the ape—or something, any-way—hurrying across an open area in the swamp. Shealy also operates Skunk-Ape Research Headquarters, which is located in Ochopee, a speck on the Tamiami Trail fifty-five miles west of Miami. That's where I'm headed today.

En route, I pass by a deserted lot on the left where there was once a tourist attraction, of which all that remains is a weathered sign that says FROG CITY. I pass some open at-tractions with Miccosukee names—Buffalo Tiger, Osceola Panther—where tourists can take airboat rides, watch alliga-tor shows, learn about nature, maybe eat some frog legs or alligator nuggets.

About thirty miles out of Miami I pass a road on the right marked by a sign that says DADE-COLLIER TRAINING AND

TRANSITION AIRPORT. This road goes to one of the more incongruous sights in the Everglades: a 10,500-foot concrete runway, capable of handling jumbo jets, surrounded by . . . nothing. The runway was built in the late sixties as part of a planned "Everglades Jetport," which was going to be the world's biggest airport, with six runways, capable of handling supersonic jets. The project was scuttled when people realized that the Everglades are unique, precious, fragile and irreplaceable, etc. But the runway is still out there. It's sometimes used for aviation training, although there are rumors of secret military operations, and occasionally a plane deemed suspicious by the authorities will be forced down there by Air Force fighters.

Every now and then, when I'm on a commercial flight descending toward Miami International Airport, we pass over the Jetport runway, and to me, especially if night is falling and I have had a couple of Bloody Marys, it always looks vaguely sinister, this huge, deserted strip of concrete in the middle of nowhere with nothing but miles of swamp around it in every direction. I imagine what it might be like at night, with gators all around, and snakes slithering off the runway to avoid mystery planes landing in the dark.

As I say, the Everglades creep me out.

I'm a little early for my appointment with Dave Shealy, so a few miles before Ochopee I stop at the Big Cypress National Preserve Visitor Center. (The National Park Service administers this part of the Everglades as a preserve.) It turns out that the visitor center is closed this morning; there's only one car other than mine in the parking lot and there's nobody in it.

There's a canal running alongside the property, separated from the parking lot by a low chain-link fence with a sign that says DO NOT FEED OR HARASS ALLIGATORS. Another sign offers some Alligator Safety Tips, including: "Fifteen feet is the recommended safe distance for alligators." This tip is illustrated by a diagram showing a silhouette of a man standing fifteen feet from the silhouette of a large alligator. The man, who appears to be wearing a suit or sport jacket, appears unconcerned: He has a relaxed, casual stance, half turned away from the alligator, as if he's not at all worried about it, seeing how he is the federally recommended distance away. The alligator, on the other hand, is looking directly at the man. Its jaws are open, revealing sharp, jagged teeth. It is clearly thinking: "That's right, don't worry about me, Mr. Sign-trusting, recommended-distance-observing, tasty-looking, sport-jacket Man."

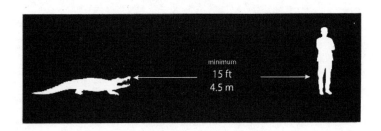

I wander over to the fence to look at the canal. On cue, an alligator roughly the size of a standard aircraft carrier slides off the opposite bank into the water. I scurry back to the car to grab my camera, then scurry back to take a picture of it. Here's the actual alligator I saw, with a UPS truck next to it for scale:

As I watch the alligator, it makes a slow left turn. It is now heading directly toward me. It can't get to me, of course, because there's a fence. I have nothing to worry about! Nevertheless, standing out there alone in the empty, silent parking lot, I feel an overpowering urge, originating from deep in my sphincter, to be somewhere else. I turn and walk briskly back to my car.

At the Big Cypress National Preserve Visitor Center, nobody can hear you scream.

I resume driving west and soon reach Ochopee, which consists of a tiny post office (billed as the smallest in the nation), a restaurant called Joannie's Crab Shack, a commercial campground, and not much else. There used to be a larger community here, but when the federal government created the Big Cypress Preserve it bought out most of the landowners (more on this later).

My destination is the campground, which is called the Trail Lakes Campground, and which is operated by Dave

Shealy and his brother Jack. The campground is also the home of Skunk-Ape Research Headquarters. Picture a scientific facility—a modern building housing pristine research laboratories equipped with the latest high-precision scientific instruments. Skunk-Ape Research Headquarters is nothing like that. It looks more like a tiki bar frequented by motorcycle gangs.

Skunk-Ape Research Headquarters also serves as the campground store. Here you can rent your campsite, book a tour, and buy snacks, supplies and souvenirs, including skunk ape T-shirts, skunk ape hoodies, skunk ape drink koozies, skunk ape hunting permits, skunk ape refrigerator magnets, bottles of skunk ape repellant and so on. If you can't find the skunk ape–related item you're looking for here, it probably doesn't exist.

Outside the headquarters, positioned semi-randomly around the property, are statues of various animals, including a gigantic Florida panther, a lion, a killer whale and a gorilla holding (why not?) the flag of Iceland.

I pull into the campground property shortly before noon and I notice that there's a turtle making its way across the parking lot, moving at the speed of a turtle. It's not as big as the alligator; it's more the size of a toaster. But it has a grumpy look to it, and I do not trust it. I get out of my car and eye it warily.

Also in the parking lot is a bearded man wearing camouflage shorts and an official Skunk-Ape Research Headquarters tank top. Apparently, he is familiar with this particular turtle. "Yesterday he was going that way," he tells me, pointing in the direction of Tampa. "Today he's going the other way."

I ask the man what kind of turtle it is. He says it's a snapping turtle. I move a little closer to snap[1] a picture of it.

"Don't get too close," the man says. "That's the fastest turtle there is, as far as striking. Lightning-fast."

---

1. Ha.

I step back from the turtle. Fortunately, it makes no attempt to strike. It continues across the parking lot, in the direction of Miami.

I chat with the bearded man, who reveals that he is Jack Shealy, the reclusive older brother of Dave. I ask him about the giant panther statue, and he tells me that not far from where we're standing a panther jumped on a motorcyclist driving on the Tamiami Trail. I wonder what the federally approved safe distance from a panther is. Probably several miles.

I ask Jack if I can take his picture and he says—politely but definitely—no. He goes off to do something with a boat and I go into Skunk-Ape Research Headquarters to examine the merchandise. I buy a black long-sleeved skunk ape shirt for my wife. The ladies love a romantic gesture.

As I'm paying for the shirt, Dave Shealy appears in the doorway. He's a tall, lean guy, fifty-two years old, with a shaved head and a gray goatee. He has startlingly blue eyes that, as a professional wordsmith, I am required to describe as "piercing." He's wearing a sleeveless Skunk-Ape Research HQ shirt, jeans and a pair of high Red Wing boots.

I will hang out with Shealy for the next four hours, most of which consist of him talking. He's smart and articulate, a good storyteller, a yarn-spinner. He can be charming, and

funny. I ask him if he's married and he says, "I was married, one time, briefly. But I've had a lot of live-in girlfriends, and, to my credit, they were all beautiful." He's currently in a relationship with a woman in Naples. He has a son who he says is financially involved in running the campground but does not live in Ochopee.

Shealy is an entrepreneur, always looking for ways to promote the campground and the skunk ape research, always thinking of new lines of business to get into. He's raising koi;

he wants to grow and sell staghorn ferns. He talks a lot about money, which he says he doesn't have much of, and the various ways he's had to hustle to survive over the years. He says that lately he's been installing swimming pool equipment in Naples, where his current lady friend lives.

Shealy is definitely a survivor. Let's say that tomorrow some apocalyptic event—a massive financial meltdown, a nuclear war, a major Facebook glitch—causes American society to collapse. Suddenly there's no food at the grocery store, no money in the ATM, no electricity in the wall sockets. There is no fire department, no medical care, no police to protect you. The world has become a violent, extremely dangerous place, a place where predators of all kinds roam the streets, and you're totally on your own, with nobody to keep you and your family alive except yourself.

I don't know about you, but I'd last maybe three days. I'd be Purina Predator Chow.

Dave Shealy would be just fine out in the Everglades. He's a member of a tough but dwindling breed of Floridians known as Gladesmen, guys who have spent their lives roaming the swamp. Shealy knows how and where to hunt deer, where to catch fish, where to net crabs. He knows where to find the biggest bullfrogs, how to spear them, skin them, chop off and cook their meaty legs. He knows places where a person can hole up. If you went looking for him, he'd see you before you saw him. He'd survive out there, come whatever. He's a survivor.

Shealy invites me back to his house. He grabs a big sack of fish food from his pickup truck and carries it out to his back deck, which overlooks a pond where he's raising koi. He dumps a bunch of food into the pond, which instantly erupts as the koi and many other fish swarm to the food, their gaping mouths breaking the surface, slurping down the food pellets. It's amazing to me how many large fish are swimming around in that murky water. If you don't like the idea of living things pretty much everywhere, you would not like the Everglades.

With the sound of fish slurping in the background, Shealy and I sit on the deck to talk. He lights the first of a half-dozen cigarettes he'll smoke that afternoon and tells me his story.

His family has been in Florida since the 1800s. His father was a machinist who worked in Miami but went out to the Everglades often to hunt and fish. He also had a side business: He made moonshine in a still he built out in the swamp. (People made moonshine in the Everglades long after Prohibition ended; I'm guessing people still do.)

In 1961, Shealy's father bought some property near the Turner River.

"He bought this land with moonshine money," says Shealy. Shealy's parents built the Trail Lakes Campground, which was where they raised Jack and Dave. Shealy's mother also served as the Ochopee postmaster; his father organized a volunteer fire department. The boys roamed the swamp freely, neighbors helped each other out, and life was good, if not always easy, in the tight little community of Ochopee.

Then, in 1974, the federal government, at the urging of environmentalists concerned about overdevelopment of the Everglades, created the Big Cypress Preserve. Suddenly the Shealys were not living in a mere swamp; they were living in an ecosystem, which had been officially deemed unique, precious, fragile, etc., and which was now to be administered by people far from Ochopee.

The law that created the Big Cypress Preserve allowed the Seminoles and Miccosukee to remain on their land and operate businesses. But the law gave the government the power to buy out non-Indian landowners who had arrived after a certain cutoff date—if necessary, by condemning their land. Some landowners fought the government, claiming their constitutional rights were being violated, but in the end the government won. Many of the Shealy family's neighbors had to leave. Ochopee turned into a ghost town.

To say that Dave Shealy is not a fan of the federal government, or environmentalists, would be an understatement. He's still bitter about what happened to Ochopee, and he's not alone. Jeff Whichello, who grew up in Ochopee, and whose family operated a motel there before being forced out of business, wrote a book called *What Happened to Ochopee?* In it, he says this about the Big Cypress land acquisition:

> *Only people with a certain creativity, work-ethic, and talent succeeded in this mucky land.... A small twentieth century pioneer town prospered on the open plain where children were born and families lived in peace.*
>
> *Then, the takers came. These big-picture people were unconcerned about the details of their actions while staring at a map of Florida from their government offices. They were unable to imagine or realize the activities of this unique community living free in the wild. When environmentalists and developers collided on the Ochopee battle ground, it was the common person, the one who scrambled every day to feed their family, who suffered in this war.*

Melodramatic, yes. But it's how some people felt then, and still feel today.

The Shealys, because they had bought their land earlier than their neighbors, were allowed to keep their campground. But over the years new regulations restricted their operations, especially airboat and swamp buggy rides, which were sources of revenue for them. Meanwhile, the park service was building new campsites nearby—free campsites—creating tough competition for Trail Lakes.

"The government wanted us gone," says Shealy.

Business at Trail Lakes suffered. "Things started to unravel," says Shealy. "It really rocked the boat in my mother and father's relationship."

Then things got worse.

"My father somehow, I don't know how, he got AIDS," says Shealy. "He passed away."

The campground was in trouble. "Money was tight," says Shealy. He pauses, lights a cigarette. Then he says, "At that time there was a lot of marijuana smuggling going on."

Indeed there was. In the late seventies and throughout the eighties, Florida was awash in marijuana and cocaine; at one point, the Florida attorney general declared that drug trafficking was the second-biggest industry in the state, behind only tourism. Bales of pot—the legendary "square groupers"—washed up on South Florida beaches. Bags of cocaine, tossed from planes by smugglers being pursued by the feds, literally fell from the sky.[2] There were absolutely insane quantities of cash floating around Miami.

A huge amount of marijuana was coming in through Everglades City, a small, close-knit community a few miles west of Ochopee on Chokoloskee Bay. Traditionally, the main trade there had been catching fish and stone crabs. But the fishermen and crabbers had found that they could make more money—a *lot* more money, in cash—using their boats, and their local knowledge, to offload pot from smugglers' ships out in the Gulf of Mexico, then bring it back through the Ten Thousand Islands, which from the air looks like the world's most complicated maze. Good luck to any outsider lawman trying to follow a local fisherman through *that* in the dark.

From Everglades City, the pot was transported by land to Miami. Which meant it was moving through Ochopee. Which presented a financial opportunity for the Shealy brothers.

"I knew what people were doing," Dave Shealy says. "We were offered money to allow them to bring marijuana across the property. My brother and I worked with the smugglers."

2. One such cocaine bag came down in the city of Homestead, where—this really happened—it interrupted a Citizens Crime Watch meeting being addressed by the chief of police. Another bag dropped from the same plane hit a church.

Shealy says they were involved in smuggling a million pounds of pot, "although we weren't caught for that much."

But they were caught. A lot of people were. In the end, the feds arrested more than three hundred people in Everglades City and nearby Chokoloskee. It was a national news story, this seemingly sleepy fishing village where it seemed as if almost everybody was involved in running drugs.

Dave Shealy served three years in the federal facility at Maxwell Air Force Base in Alabama. His mother died thirty days before he got out. He returned to Ochopee, and to the struggle of keeping the campground afloat. This is when the skunk ape—which he says he first saw when he was ten—became a major part of his life.

"When I got home from prison, there was a rash of sightings," he says. He cites anecdotes about tourists who told him they'd seen the ape, including two women who were photographing bromeliads on Turner River Road—where many alleged sightings have occurred—and encountered the skunk ape when they returned to their car.

"What was unusual about that one," says Shealy, "is that it had an erection."

Shealy created Skunk-Ape Research Headquarters and started doing his "research": putting out skunk ape bait—mainly lima beans—and finding footprints, from which he made plaster casts. He wrote the *Skunk Ape Research Field Guide* and made a DVD. He told tourists about the ape and talked tirelessly to the media, doing interview after interview, spreading the word. More tourists came to Ochopee looking for the ape, and more media people. There were more sightings.

Of course there were also plenty of skeptics. There still are—people who see Dave Shealy as a huckster making crap up to sell his skunk ape merchandise. I ask Shealy about this.

"The skeptics have never been here," he says. "For them to say it doesn't exist, it's just absurd. The frightening thing is, their ignorance can be pushing a species into extinction. I know that it's real. It's a real live animal."

So there you are.

Shealy and I talk on his back porch for about an hour. Then we get into his truck to tour the area. He shows me around the Trail Lakes Campground, a peaceful, pleasant patch of land that offers campsites and "chickees," which are little raised, thatched, screened-in cabins patterned after Indian dwellings. Then he takes me to a spot looking out toward where he says he first saw the skunk ape, when he was ten. It's a story he has told many times.

"I heard something walking in the water," he says. But he

couldn't see it because the grass was too high. His brother Jack lifted him up to see.

"Here's this animal, walking through the grass," he says. "It was covered with hair, but it wasn't like a bear. It was like a person."

I take a picture of Shealy, pointing toward where he saw the skunk ape. I get the feeling he's done this same pose in this same spot a hundred times.

We get back in the truck, and Shealy takes me on a tour of Greater Ochopee. We head out on a back road where Shealy says he's seen a large python, which he'd like to catch. I ask him how a person catches a large python.

"You grab it by the tail," he says.

We don't (thank God) find a python, but we do see a park ranger. Shealy stops the truck and yells to him.

"We're skunk ape hunting," he yells. "Any tips on where there might be a skunk ape?"

The ranger, looking uncomfortable, says no, he has no information on that. Shealy, clearly enjoying the ranger's discomfort, grins and drives away.

We head over to Everglades City, which is back to being a fishing village, and continue a few miles south to Chokoloskee, a small community on an island at the mouth of the Turner River. We stop at the Smallwood Cemetery, a tiny, semi-hidden plot of ground with a few dozen gravestones, some old, some fairly recent. One of them marks the grave of one of Shealy's ancestors. It says:

**ATKA SHEALY**

**BORN 10 AUG 1869—DIED 15 JAN 1901**

**SHE WAS THE WIFE OF W. G. SHEALY**

We drive around Chokoloskee, then Everglades City, Shealy waving to people, some of whom he says he smuggled drugs with. Everybody seems to know him. Then we head back in the Preserve. We turn off the Tamiami Trail now, driving on back roads made from hardpacked sand and shell dredgings. Shealy points to places where his neighbors' homes once stood, now wild and overgrown, taken back by the swamp.

We pass an isolated house that's still standing but abandoned. Shealy tells me it used to be occupied by a strange man, a loner, who kept wolves as pets.

"I'd be out at night, hunting," he says. "I could hear those wolves howling."

The thing was, nobody could figure out what the man was feeding the wolves. But there were rumors. People said the man would drive to Miami in his van, pick up homeless people and prostitutes there. They would never be seen again.

As Shealy tells me this, I'm looking at the house. The day is sunny, the temperature is over 90, and I'm getting chills.

"There's a lot of missing people," says Shealy.

We turn onto Turner River Road, which is where a number of skunk ape sightings have occurred over the years. My sense is that at this point in the ritual Kabuki Theater of skunk ape journalism, we are supposed to be looking for the skunk ape. My role here is to be the skeptical but bemused reporter, asking questions; Shealy's role is to be Mr. Skunk Ape, showing me places where this group of tourists or that group of hunters spotted the ape; where he found footprints; where he set out lima beans that were mysteriously gone the next day.

But I'm feeling too old for Kabuki Theater. I don't ask any more questions. We ride in silence. After a while, Shealy, gamely playing his role, says, "So, I suppose you want to know if the skunk ape is real."

"Not really," I say.

This answer seems to surprise him. But after a second or two he plunges ahead, delivering his lines.

"The Seminoles believe the skunk ape lives inside the Earth," he says. "You can only see it if it wants you to. Some say it's a spirit. But what I saw is flesh and blood."

I write that down in my notebook but ask no more questions. We drive back to Skunk-Ape Research Headquarters. We shake hands and he's gone. I get back into my car and drive back to Miami, probably passing the snapping turtle that was also headed that way.

Two days later I get an email from Shealy:

I had a great time! nice meeting you THANKS

I email him back that I also enjoyed spending the afternoon with him. And I really did. Shealy is a smart, informed, genuinely interesting person.

For the record, I don't believe the skunk ape is real. I believe that if there were such a thing, somebody would have taken a decent picture of it by now since everybody in the world has a phone with a pretty good camera.

Does this mean I think Dave Shealy is a hoaxer?

No, I think he's a survivor. I actually think he's done a pretty wonderful thing, out there in the swamp, keeping Ochopee on the map. And I don't think he's doing anybody any harm, especially not compared to other people making money off of things I don't think are real. For example, I think astrology is a massive pile of bullshit. Likewise, feng shui. I don't believe "mediums" can communicate with dead people. I don't believe the miraculous claims made by most major religions. At funerals, when the clergyperson says the deceased has gone to a better place, I don't believe it, and I don't think the clergyperson always believes it either.

So I'm not going to get worked up over the skunk ape.

I'm not a scientist, and I don't know who's right about how the Everglades should be protected. I think it's probably a good thing that development has been stopped out there. But I think the federal government could have done a much better job of dealing with the landowners, and especially grasping the fact that Ochopee was a real community that—like the Miccosukee and the Seminoles—deserved some protection.

It's too late for Ochopee. But it's not too late for Skunk-Ape Research Headquarters. I think it would be nice if the National Park Service developed a sense of humor and recognized the headquarters as some kind of official historic thing, to be preserved as a classic example of a traditional, quintessentially Florida cultural icon: The Sketchy Roadside Attraction.

I also think it would be wonderful if the government recognized that Dave Shealy is an endangered species. I think he should be protected, not unlike the way the Florida panther is protected, except that it would be a very big mistake to try to put a radio collar on Dave Shealy.

None of this will happen, of course. It's a good bet that, sooner or later, Skunk-Ape Research Headquarters will be just another ghost attraction on the Tamiami Trail, like Frog City. So if you want to see it, I recommend you see it soon. Afterward, you can check out the Everglades, which—make no mistake—are a unique, precious, etc. Be sure to wear mosquito repellant. I'll wave to you as I drive past.

# WEEKI WACHEE
## AND
# SPONGEORAMA

For thousands of years, two legendary mythical creatures have drawn men to the sea:

1. Mermaids.
2. Sponges.

I have heard the seductive siren song of these creatures, which is all the more amazing when you consider that sponges do not have mouths. And so it is that on a bright fall Florida day I find myself driving north from the Tampa Airport, across the Pithlachascotee River, to the place where

Route 50 meets Route 19. This is the town of Weeki Wachee, which has a population of four,[1] and which is known as The City of Mermaids. It is the home of Weeki Wachee Springs, which, of all the classic Florida roadside tourist attractions, is one of the Florida-est.

It began as the dream of a man named Newton "Newt" Perry, who was raised in nearby Ocala. Perry was a gifted swimmer—sometimes called The Human Fish—who could hold his breath for as long as eight minutes. He put on swimming exhibitions in which he performed tricks such as eating bananas underwater, which is a handy skill because, as you can imagine, after several minutes of being submerged, a person gets hungry. Perry was a consultant on movies involving underwater scenes, including *Creature from the Black Lagoon*, the horror classic about a scientific expedition to the Amazon that is terrorized by a man wearing an uncomfortable rubber suit.

In the mid-forties, Perry had the idea of building an underwater theater at Weeki Wachee, which is the deepest natural spring in the United States, producing 117 million gallons of fresh water *every single day*. It's almost impossible to imagine that much water gushing up out of the earth un-

---

1. Really.

less you have lived in a house I once owned in Pennsylvania, which had a basement that was highly susceptible to flooding. It was a nightmare. I could hear whales calling to each other down there. One difference between Newt Perry and me, aside from our relative breath-holding abilities, is that when I looked at my basement, I never thought: "Hey, that could be a tourist attraction!"

But Newt had that kind of vision, and in 1947 he opened Weeki Wachee, with its underwater theater, to the public. The audience sat on rows of benches facing a wide glass wall, on the other side of which attractive young women in bathing suits performed aquatic ballet and did tricks, including eating and drinking underwater. Instead of surfacing to breathe or wearing scuba tanks, the performers inhaled compressed air from rubber hoses, which they'd drop onto an underwater platform and pick up as needed.

According to Weeki Wachee lore, in the early days, when the performers heard a car coming, they'd run out to Route 19 in their swimsuits and try to lure the driver into the parking lot; if they got a customer—even just one—they'd put on a show. By the 1950s, more tourists were coming, and the performers—now called mermaids—were wearing tails.

Weeki Wachee hit the big time in 1959, when the American Broadcasting Company bought the spring, enlarged the theater, upgraded the facilities and began using Weeki Wachee as a filming location. It was now a major tourist attraction and it drew big-name entertainers such as Elvis, Don Knotts and Arthur Godfrey. (It seems as if every account of Weeki Wachee's glory days mentions this trio of celebrities.) Large crowds came throughout the sixties; Weeki Wachee became known around the world; the mermaids were famous. Times were good.

And then, in the seventies (cue scary music—specifically, "It's a Small World"), Disney came to Florida. Suddenly the Weeki Wachee mermaids, with their tails and their air hoses and their display of underwater eating, were competing with a space roller coaster, a pirate ride, a fairy-tale castle, a haunted mansion, fireworks, beloved characters walking around wearing giant heads, turkey legs and much more (including mermaids).

Florida tourism started to change. Visitors no longer meandered along the state's byways, stopping for a few hours at whatever roadside attraction caught their eye, then moving on to the next one. Now they went straight to the Magic Kingdom, which sucked them into its powerful gravitational Fun Vortex and held them there, like a black hole with Jiminy Cricket.

Over the next few decades, attendance at Weeki Wachee

declined. The park changed hands several times and fell into disrepair. By 2001, it was in danger of going out of business. It was saved by the fund-raising efforts of current and former mermaids, who got local businesses to help out. Then in 2008 the state of Florida, seeking to save an iconic part of the state's tourism culture, stepped in and made Weeki Wachee Springs an official state park. This meant that Weeki Wachee's future was secure. It also meant that the mermaids became state employees, which I think is wonderful. As a Florida resident, I would much rather see my tax money spent on mermaids than on, for example, the lieutenant governor.

Today Weeki Wachee is alive and well, although on the day I arrive—a Tuesday in October, not a prime time for tourism—the parking lot is mostly empty. I pay my $13 admission, go inside and look around.

Let's get this out of the way: If you are looking for high-octane excitement, or even medium-octane excitement, Weeki Wachee is not for you. It is low-key, bordering on sleepy. It's like the fifties never ended in there. Walking around, I almost expect to see a dad in plaid Bermudas using his Kodak Brownie to take snapshots of his wife, Betty, and their two kids, Billy and Sally, before they head home in their '57 Chevy Bel Air to watch Elvis, Don Knotts and Arthur Godfrey on their Philco black-and-white TV.

In fact, most of the people I see at Weeki Wachee are retired couples, plus a few families with preschool children,
strolling around and checking out the park. Aside from the
underwater theater, there's a water park with slides, animal
exhibits, a gift shop with many mermaid-themed items, a
restaurant, canoe and kayak rentals, playgrounds, etc. Weeki
Wachee also has the one essential element you look for in a
true classic Florida tourist attraction: a Mold-A-Matic.

A Mold-A-Matic is a machine traditionally found at older
Florida tourist attractions. You feed in some money—these
days, usually $2—and, thanks to the miracle of plastic injec-

tion molding, nothing happens, because traditionally the Mold-A-Matic—the one at Weeki Wachee, for example—is out of order. On those occasions when it does work, the Mold-A-Matic produces, after some chugging and hissing, a fresh-baked, still-warm little plastic souvenir related to whatever attraction you are visiting. The Weeki Wachee machine, theoretically, cranks out a mermaid.

Speaking of needing maintenance: Weeki Wachee has let itself go a little. Some of the buildings could use fresh paint and the grass needs cutting. If this were a Disney property, the head groundskeeper would be beheaded as an example to the staff. On the other hand, if this were a Disney property, they'd charge you a hell of a lot more than $13 to get in. For $13, you could maybe buy a Disney pretzel.

I pass the water park, Buccaneer Bay, and amble down to the Wilderness River Cruise. This is a pontoon-boat ride on the Weeki Wachee River, which is formed by the water gushing out of the spring and flows seven miles to the Gulf of Mexico. As I board the boat with maybe two dozen other tourists, the guide makes a few well-rehearsed jokes about feeding us to the alligators and we chuckle, because that is our role. Then we shove off for our Wilderness Cruise on the mighty Weeki Wachee.

To continue the Disney comparison: The comparable ride

in the Magic Kingdom is the Jungle Cruise, where your guide emits a steady stream of glib comical patter ("I'd like to take a moment to point out some of the plants to you. There's one, there's one . . .") and your boat encounters many animated wildlife units, including a python, gorillas, lions, a rhinoceros and a hippo that "charges" your boat.

The Weeki Wachee Wilderness Cruise is considerably less dramatic. We don't encounter any alligators, although we do see some mullet, and, in their defense, they are actual, biological, non-animatronic mullet. The guide tells us that he has seen a young manatee hanging around. A few minutes later, we spot him, or possibly her, and we take numerous pictures.

The manatee is a largish animal, but, unlike the Jungle Cruise hippo, it does not attack our boat. Mainly what manatees do, in my experience,[2] is eat and fart. They are the adolescent boys of the marine world. Still, this manatee, like the mullet, is real, and it is definitely the highlight of the Wilderness Cruise. We turn around and head back to the dock, having spent a total of twenty minutes in the wilderness, completely isolated from any trace of civilization except for when we passed the canoe-and-kayak rental concession.

From the Wilderness Cruise, I head to the main attraction of Weeki Wachee, the Newton Perry Underwater Mermaid Theatre.

2. Yes, I have manatee experience.

There I meet up with John Athanson, a native Floridian who's the public relations manager for the park. When I find him he's talking with some movie people, who are on location filming part of a film that will be called *City of Mermaids*. Athanson tells me that the day before, for a different film shoot, the Travelocity Gnome was at the park, in person; other celebrities who have visited during Athanson's tenure include Paris Hilton and Larry the Cable Guy. Perhaps these are not names of the same caliber as Elvis, Don Knotts and, of course, Arthur Godfrey, but the point is that Weeki Wachee still has some star power.

While we're talking, an attractive blond woman approaches Athanson to discuss some mermaid-show business. This is Nikki Chickonski, who has been a mermaid for eleven years, having started as an eighteen-year-old high school student. She's joined by another woman connected with the show, who is carrying some sequined tops, and the two of them have a brief discussion about the mermaids' costumes. Chickonski informs me that they can choose from a variety of tails.

"Before the show," she says, "we'll say, Hey, what tails are we wearing?" Then they choose their tops, as certain tops go better with certain tails. "Also some tops work better on some mermaids than others," she says. "Some girls are bustier than others."

*Mermaid Nikki Chickonski, holding a mermaid top.*

Chickonski says it takes a lot of training to become a Weeki Wachee mermaid. The water is chilly—always 74.2

degrees—and the mermaids, performing fifteen to twenty feet below the surface, have to contend with the five-mile-an-hour current gushing up from the spring opening sixty-five feet below.

"We have a long training process," she says. "At first, you don't wear a tail. You train on the air hose with your legs together." The next step is a training tail: "It's different from a show tail. The training tail has a zipper, so if you need to, you can escape."

After Chickonski leaves, Athanson walks me down into the theater, which can seat 450 people, although at the moment it's almost empty. It's cool down there, out of the daytime glare; the sunlight filtering through the springwater fills the room with a bluish glow.

On the other side of the glass, some trainee mermaids are practicing, without tails, on the air hoses. Also some fish are swimming around, acting like it is no big deal to be under-water. It's a peaceful scene, and Athanson, a veteran p.r. guy, takes the opportunity to sing the praises of the spring, and take a little shot at Disney.

"This is an iconic show," he says. "You have this beautiful, peaceful spring. Then you throw in a pretty girl in a mermaid tail. It's magic. We don't need animatronics."

Around 2:30 p.m., people start drifting into the theater for the 3 o'clock mermaid show. The glass wall is now covered by a blue curtain; calypso music is playing. By 3, there are about sixty people in the audience. To warm us up for the show, TV monitors on the side walls display a Jimmy Buffett stadium concert performance of the song "Fins" featuring a quartet of seated Weeki Wachee mermaids being wheeled onto the stage. Then the blue curtain rises and, finally, we see three of them swimming gracefully into view: Elvis, Don Knotts and Arthur Godfrey.

No, seriously, what you see is three women in mermaid tops and tails. They swim around a bit, then pick up their air hoses and begin a synchronized routine, twirling, flipping, rising, falling, taking breaths from their hoses, emitting clouds of bubbles and always—*always*—smiling.

They lip-sync to a mermaid song ("We're not like other women / Fighting traffic on the shore..."). Then, responding to prompts from a recorded narrator, one of them drinks a

beverage from a bottle while another one eats an apple. We applaud these feats (we've been told the performers can hear us). Several times the mermaids perform their signature move, grabbing each other's tails and swimming in a vertical circle.

Each time, this maneuver gets a big hand. But the audience saves its most enthusiastic response for the last part of the act, "A Tribute to Our Country." We hear Lee Greenwood singing "Proud to Be an American" as two women—without tails—swim into view wearing red-white-and-blue star-spangled swimsuits. They do some patriotic synchronized swimming maneuvers, and then, for the grand finale, a mermaid (with tail) swims up from the depths of the spring holding an American flag.

This gets a big hand, including from me. Call me a proud American, if you want, but I truly believe that no other nation on Earth possesses the capability to put on a more powerful display of underwater mermaid patriotism.

After the show, some audience members press close to the glass wall to take photos of and selfies with one of the mermaids.

Other audience members go to the theater lobby to pose with a mermaid sitting on a chair.

I walk back out into the sunlight, trying to decide what I think about Weeki Wachee. I conclude that, by modern

theme-park standards, it is dated, hokey and unsophisticated. In other words, it's great. I mean that sincerely. Weeki Wachee is a time machine that takes you back to a different era. I'm not saying it was in all ways a *better* era. But it was definitely a calmer one. And for just thirteen bucks, you can go back there and mellow out for a day. Using the standard Florida Tourist Attraction Rating System, by which an attraction is rated on a scale of 1 to 5 out-of-order Mold-A-

Matics, I would give Weeki Wachee a solid 3½ out-of-order
Mold-A-Matics.

I leave Weeki Wachee, returning to the twenty-first century, and set out southbound on Route 19. If you had to select one stretch of road to validate every negative stereotype
about Florida culture, you would be hard put to do better than Route 19, which is a cavalcade of strip bars, porn
stores, pawn shops, trailer parks and billboards for personal-
injury lawyers. As a bonus, this stretch of Route 19 was
once declared by *Dateline NBC* to be the most dangerous
road in America because of the high number of pedestrian
deaths.

But there is a bright spot on Route 19. In Spring Hill, a few
miles south of Weeki Wachee on the east side of the highway,
there is a twenty-two-foot-tall, fifty-eight-foot-long bright
pink concrete dinosaur.

*Why?* you might ask. According to the Hernando County
Historical Society, the dinosaur was created in 1962 by Au-

gust Herwede, "who was a local artist that became famous back in the 1950's and early 1960's for constructing concrete dinosaur attractions along various highways in West Florida." Originally, the dinosaur was intended to attract people to a wildlife museum, but that closed because of poor attendance. It was replaced, according to the Historical Society, by a taxidermy shop that "featured over 1,200 stuffed animals which featured a prominent deformity of one kind or another." Today the dinosaur stands in front of a candy store called Fudge Factory USA.

I stop to take a picture, but do not linger, because I have to get to the sponges.[3] Still, I find the dinosaur to be visually

---

3. I bet you forgot about the sponges.

impressive, plus it has been declared a Historical Site, plus it is convenient to fudge. So I award it a Florida Tourist Attraction rating of 1½ out-of-order Mold-A-Matics.

I resume my southbound journey on the deadly Route 19, somehow managing not to hit a single pedestrian before I reach my destination, Tarpon Springs. This is the U.S. Sponge Capital, the heart of our vital domestic natural-sponge industry. This industry is dominated by Greek-Americans, whose ancestors came here in the early twentieth century to harvest sponges in the Gulf of Mexico. Today, Tarpon Springs has the highest percentage of Greek-American residents of any American city. It's a quaint and scenic little town on the water, dotted with authentic Greek restaurants and stores featuring sponges and sponge-related merchandise out the wazoo.

My destination is the granddaddy of all sponge-related attractions: Spongeorama.

Spongeorama is a combination store and museum devoted to sponges. I go into the museum part first, because—like too many Americans—I have never really given much thought to sponges. I, frankly, don't even know what a sponge is. If I had to guess, I would say it's a kind of plant.

The sponge museum is in the back of the store and it consists of a group of dusty, yellowing exhibits dating back to, I would estimate, roughly the time of Plato. Nevertheless, they are informative, and I learn many sponge facts.

To begin with, sponges are not plants. They are multi-celled animals, although they have no mouths, internal organs, brains or nervous systems. They cannot move, but they can reproduce, eat, grow and obtain Florida driver's licenses.

I'm kidding about that last one, sort of.

There are a number of ways to harvest sponges, including a method called harpooning, which conjures up an image of a brave sponge hunter, out on the sea, doing battle with his nemesis, Moby-Sponge. In fact, harpooning involves using a pole to hook the sponge off the seabed and bring it into the boat. A riskier method is to go down to the seabed personally, wearing a diving suit and helmet attached to an air hose. The Spongeorama museum, quoting *Newsweek*, says that this method of sponge hunting is probably the country's "most dangerous occupation."[4] Illustrating this point is a gruesome diorama of a diver lying on a deck, either unconscious or dead, with blood coming out of his nose.

There are many more exhibits, and many more sponge facts. For example, there is a sponge mentioned in the Bible. Really. It's the part where Jesus dies.[5]

After touring the museum, I go back into the store area,

---

4. It is the Route 19 of occupations.

5. John, Chapter 19, Verse 29: *Now there was set a vessel full of vinegar: and they filled a sponge with vinegar, and put it upon hyssop, and put it to his mouth.*

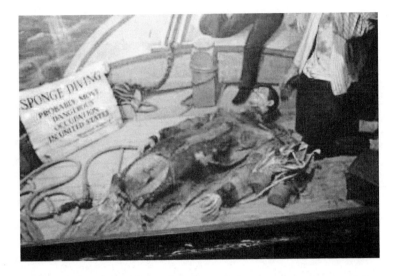

where I encounter a forceful Greek woman Spongeorama employee who tells me I should watch the movie. Far be it from me to generalize about Greek women, but in my experience they do not tend to be shrinking violets. If a Greek woman tells you to do something, you do it.

The forceful Greek woman directs me and some other tourists into a side room with benches and a movie screen. She informs us that the movie is "very historical," then turns on the projector and leaves.

The movie appears to be a few decades old, done in the style of the documentaries you watched in middle school when you had a substitute teacher, with titles like *The Story of Baking Soda*. The soundtrack quavers, and the colors are murky, tending toward purple and red, as if the scenes were filmed through a pitcher of Kool-Aid.

The protagonist is a guy—I will call him Spongeorama Man—who presents a detailed explanation of how sponges are processed for sale to the consumer. I would strongly recommend this film for anybody thinking of going into sponge-processing as a career, because Spongeorama Man is extremely thorough, to the point where I am in danger of nodding off. But I perk up when he starts talking about the various types of sponges for sale at Spongeorama, because I know that when I leave this room, I am going to have no choice but to purchase a sponge from the forceful Greek woman, and I need to know which kind I should get.

This turns out to be a more complicated decision than you might think. At first I lean toward getting a yellow sponge, which Spongeorama Man states is "an excellent all-purpose sponge." I reject the finger sponge, which is mainly for florists and aquariums, although Spongeorama Man says "the fish enjoy it." I also pass on the flowerpot sponge,[6] which you grow plants in.

The sponge I settle on is the wool sponge. "This is the Cadillac of sponges," states Spongeorama Man. "If you're look-

---

6. I am not making any of these sponges up.

ing for a top-grade sponge, this is it." At this point, I am sold; I'm going to splurge on a wool sponge as a gift for my wife. The ladies love a romantic gesture.

I'm all set to leave the theater and buy a wool sponge when Spongeorama Man, instead of ending the movie, introduces *another* movie, which is longer, older and murkier than the first one. In terms of production values, it makes the first film look like *Star Wars: The Force Awakens*. It's a documentary, with a dramatic narrator, about Greek men heading out on ships and smoking cigarettes and harvesting sponges and just generally being very Greek. In one of the more dramatic moments, we see a man haul a freshly caught sponge into the boat, and we finally get a chance to see a live, pre-processing sponge close up. It looks—and I say this as a person who has nothing but the deepest respect for the sponge as an organism—like a turd.

We also see scenes of a diver in a helmet and canvas suit collecting sponges on the seafloor while dramatic music plays in the background. If, at that moment, a Weeki Wachee mermaid swam past the diver holding an American flag, it would be the greatest documentary ever made. Unfortunately, that does not happen. Instead, the film goes into a stirring, surreal finale in which the announcer dramatically lists all the wonderful uses of sponges while, in the background, a dramatic chorus—it might even be Greek—chants, over and over, "Real sponges! Natural sponges!"

By the time the movie ends, I am fired up and ready to make my sponge purchase. I go back into the store, where I am confronted by a bewildering array of sponges, loofas[7] and other products.

The forceful Greek woman approaches me. I tell her I want to buy my wife a wool sponge, but I don't know which one. Without hesitating, she picks up a sponge and hands it to me. "Your wife wants this one," she says, forcefully. She can tell just by *looking* at me which sponge my wife wants.

---

7. According to Spongeorama Man, a loofa is not a sponge. It is a vegetable.

I pay for the sponge. It costs $23, which sounds like a lot until you consider that it is the Cadillac of sponges. It comes with a sheet of instructions titled HOW TO CARE FOR YOUR NATURAL SPONGE. I am confident that my wife will be thrilled.

So I'm in a fairly positive mood as I leave Spongeorama. It's not as pleasant or elaborate as Weeki Wachee, but it is an attraction that combines an educational experience with an opportunity to purchase quality household products. After some deliberation, I decide to award it 2 out of 5 out-of-order Mold-A-Matics.

If you're in the Tarpon Springs area, you should definitely stop in, check out the museum and catch the movie. And if you're in the market for a quality natural sponge, your search is over: I'll sell you the one I got for my wife.

# CASSADAGA

It's a week before Halloween and I'm checking into the Hotel Cassadaga. It's the only hotel in Cassadaga, Florida, a community with a population of a few hundred, unless you count the spirits of the dead, in which case it's about the same size as L.A.

Cassadaga is, literally, a ghost town. It was founded in 1894 by a man named George Colby, who belonged to the Spiritualist Movement, which believes that when you die, your spirit lives on and people can communicate with you through mediums. There's still a Spiritualist community in Cassadaga, centered on the Cassadaga Spiritualist Camp; around it has grown a small industry of mediums and psychics, which is why Cassadaga's nickname is The Psychic Capital of the World. As you drive into town on Cassadaga Road, you pass house after house with signs that say PSYCHIC.

This is a place where you might have trouble getting a plumber on the weekend, but if you need an emergency tarot card reading, help is only seconds away.

The Cassadaga Hotel is across the street from the Spiritualist Camp Welcome Center in the heart of downtown Cassadaga. On the day I arrive at the hotel it is doing its best to look creepy, having been festooned with fake spiderwebs, skeletons, skulls, etc., for Halloween. In Cassadaga, Halloween is, basically, Christmas.

The hotel was built in the 1920s and it still looks like the 1920s inside. The lobby has been spookified for Halloween, with a skeleton seated on a banquette.

The hotel check-in counter is a desk inside the gift shop. A nice lady checks me in and tells me that I will be staying in Room 2. She also tells me that the hotel is haunted. I ask her how the ghosts manifest themselves.

"They may pet you like a kitty cat," she says. "They may move your glasses. They may move your key."

A woman nearby, shopping for gifts, nods her head.

"They definitely will," she says.

I head for my room. It's on a narrow, dimly lit, creepy hallway that's straight out of the Haunted Mansion ride at Disney World, except it's real. I can easily imagine an evil entity lurking behind one of the doors, preparing to spring out at me with an ax, or a knife, or a live lobster.[1]

I enter Room 2 without incident. It's a modest room with an old-fashioned four-poster bed and a window air conditioner with the fan set on "Typhoon." There's no TV set, no Wi-Fi. It is probably for the best. If the spirits of the departed are, in fact, hovering all around, they'd probably be angry if you started looking at television or a laptop. They'd be, like, "I've been sitting around dead all these years and you finally show up and the first thing you do is *go on Facebook*?"

I spend a few minutes in my room, waiting for ghosts to

---

1. I'm afraid of lobsters.

tickle me like a kitty cat or move my keys, but nothing happens. This is understandable; it's their busy season.

I head across the street to the Spiritualist Camp Welcome Center. It has a big bookstore and gift shop, offering a wide selection of New Age-y books, candles, incense, tarot cards, crystals and T-shirts, among many other spiritual items; there are bulletin boards cluttered with flyers advertising healing circles, mediumship classes, spirit encounters, etc.

Off to the side is a room where you can make an appointment with a medium. The way it works is, the mediums write their names and phone numbers on a whiteboard, and you call the one you want to meet. A sign says "We can't recommend which one you should call. Use your intuition in selecting a medium." There's an ATM machine right there in case your medium doesn't accept credit cards.

Using my intuition, I start at the top of the list. After getting several voicemail machines, I reach a live medium, whom I will call Judy. She tells me she just had a cancellation, so she has an availability right away. She says the session will last thirty to forty-five minutes and will cost $60, in cash.

Following Judy's directions, I walk a few blocks to a small house on a side street. Judy, a plump woman in (I'm guessing) her thirties, ushers me through a kitchen to a darkened living room where candles are burning and New Age music is playing softly. She has me sit on a sofa; she sits on a chair in front of me, with a small table between us.

Judy tells me a little about the history of Cassadaga and explains that she is a trained medium, affiliated with the Spiritualist Camp. She says she doesn't use "tools" such as tarot cards. In Cassadaga, the mediums, who claim they can communicate with the dead, tend to look down on the psychics, who use cards, crystals and other items, and who claim they have the ability to see into the future, among other powers.

Judy produces a sheet of paper and says she will be writing down things as she goes so I'll have a record of our session. She writes my name in large letters on the paper and begins talking. As she speaks, she often looks past me, as if she's seeing a spirit I can't see. Sometimes she talks to the spirit. "Thank you," she'll say.

Judy says she's seeing canisters and asks if that has any significance to me. I try to think of canisters that have been significant in my life, but nothing comes to mind. To be honest, I can go for months without thinking of canisters. Judy says it might have something to do with oil or an auto shop, and that "placement" is important. She goes on for a while, talking about the placement of the canisters, but it's not ringing any bells. I'm starting to feel bad, like I'm letting Judy and the spirit community down.

Judy says she's seeing the number 76. I wrack my brain, but all I can come up with is the song "Seventy-six Trombones," which is a rousing show tune but not one with which I feel a deep personal connection. I shake my head.

Judy says she's picking up something about bowling balls and brings up "placement" again. I shake my head again; I'm not a bowler. I am totally failing at this.

Judy asks me if I have trouble eating.

"I wish," I say. This is turning into a nightmare.

Judy says she's getting something about a woman who maybe has something to do with race cars.

I shake my head again. My wife happens to be a woman, and she is a fast driver, but not of race cars. She's an SUV woman. I'm beginning to think the dead people Judy's talking to have me confused with somebody else.

Then Judy says she's getting something about turkey.

"The bird or the country?" I ask.

"The bird," she says.

"I like turkey," I say.

Judy seems pleased. I feel relieved. Finally, we're getting somewhere!

Judy says she's getting something about music. I tell her I'm in a band. This is true: I'm in an author rock band called the Rock Bottom Remainders. We are not *good* at music, but we do attempt to play it.

Judy asks about the name Ron. I tell her my wife's cousin's husband is named Ron. We are on a roll now, spiritually. We are 3 for 3.

Then Judy brings up my parents. "Have they transitioned?" she says.

"Have they what?" I say.

"Died," she says.

I tell her they have, in fact, transitioned. She asks me if I would like to try to contact them via a Spirit Box, which she says is a device that enables the dead to communicate with us. I say sure. She goes to a closet and brings back a small electronic device, which she connects to a tiny speaker. She explains that the Spirit Box picks up radio transmissions, and the spirits "piggyback" on these transmissions to say things to us.

She tells me she's going to record me asking some "validating questions" to prove that it's my parents I'm connecting with. Speaking into the Spirit Box, I ask a few questions, like where my parents were born and what street I grew up on. Then we go through a process wherein Judy plays back my questions and we both listen intently to the Spirit Box, trying to pick out messages from beyond as the box emits static, random sounds and fragments of radio broadcasts. To you, this probably sounds like a load of hooey, but I can state for a fact, as a person who witnessed it firsthand, that you are absolutely correct: It is a large, steaming, fragrant pile of hooey. I have a hard time keeping a straight face. Judy would say, "Did you hear that?" And I'd say, "What?" And she'd say, "It sounded like 'love you.' Listen." Then she'd play a staticky random sound that could have been "love you," but also could have been "trampoline," "fester," "dirigible," "Neil Sedaka," "Montpelier" or pretty much anything else, and I'd go, "Huh."

We do that for a while, Judy hearing my parents telling me that they're happy being dead and they love me, me hearing static. Finally, mercifully, our session ends. I pay Judy and leave with the piece of paper on which she has written notes about canisters, placement, etc.

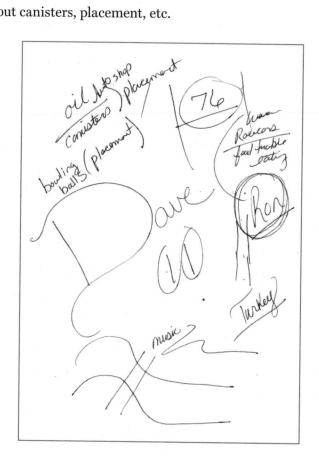

As I walk away, I find myself thinking about my parents. They both had excellent senses of humor, and they would have been immensely entertained by the Spirit Box. So I guess in a way Judy did connect me with them. It was totally worth $60.

I spend the next hour walking around the Spiritualist Camp, which is actually picturesque, consisting mostly of older wooden buildings. It reminds me a little of Key West, if Key West was inhabited by mediums and spirits instead of drunk people and even drunker people. It's a beautiful day, but even in bright sunshine Cassadaga has a creepy vibe. It's very quiet and I see zero children. There are signs everywhere reminding you that the main industry here is death.

I leave the camp and head over to the psychic side of the street, which is a little more lively. I pass a store with a sign that says WE HAVE GHOST HUNTING EQUIPMENT, then see a place called the Purple Rose, which offers, among many other services, psychic pet readings.

I go inside, where a psychic I will call Rev. Janet (the Purple Rose psychics use "Rev.") tells me she can do the reading from a photograph. She says this will cost $25. I pay her—the Purple Rose takes credit cards—then find a picture of my dog, Lucy, on my mobile phone. I hand the phone to Rev. Janet, who puts it on a machine that takes a photo of the photo and produces a Polaroid-like print of Lucy with weird colors around her head, representing her aura.

Rev. Janet leads me into an office, where we sit. She looks at Lucy's aura photo and tells me what it reveals about her. Here are her observations:

"She's very spiritual."

"She's very smart."

"She loves her owners very much."

"She doesn't like being alone."

"She's got a lot of passion and energy."

In short, to summarize what Lucy's aura reveals, as seen by a professional in the psychic field: *Lucy is a dog.*

After several minutes, Rev. Janet starts looking behind me, the same way Judy the medium did.

"There's an older woman," she says. "Is your mother alive?"

I answer no.

"Well, she's here right now," says Rev. Janet. "And she loves this dog."

My mom is *all over* Cassadaga.

Rev. Janet tells me that Lucy and my mom are great friends. "Your mother comes to visit the dog late at night. She plays with the dog from the other side."

I am frankly surprised by this. The only game Lucy likes to play is the one where she prances up to you with a filthy, saliva-soaked chew toy in her mouth and you—pretending that you find this disgusting thing as desirable as she does—make a halfhearted grab for it, and she prances away, victorious. This does not strike me as an activity that my mom would visit a dog nightly to engage in.

Of course, I'm no psychic.

I leave the Purple Rose and head back to the hotel. I have dinner in the hotel restaurant, a friendly Italian place called

Sinatra's, with decent food, a genial older crowd and a piano player doing Billy Joel tunes.

After dinner, I go back out for a stroll. It's dark now and the streets are deserted. I'm the only person walking around. It is extremely quiet. Cassadaga is definitely creepier at night. I'm reassured by the thought that my mom is around to protect me from the other spirits. Unless, of course, she's down in Miami battling Lucy for the chew toy.

I wander down the street to the Spiritualist Camp church, which is called the Colby Memorial Temple. I stand in the open doorway, looking in. There are a couple dozen people seated at the front of the church, attending a mediumship class conducted by a man with a hypnotic voice. He's telling them to picture themselves on a pathway with flowers on

both sides. He wants them to decide what flowers to pick. It's very relaxing, listening to this man. He's making me realize something, something that I have been denying, but something that I now must face: I'm sleepy.

I walk back to the Hotel Cassadaga, which at night has lighting that gives it an even spookier aura.

I pass by the lobby skeleton and enter the creepy hallway with evil entities possibly lurking behind the doors. I quickly enter Room 2 and close the door. I have to leave early tomorrow morning, so I decide to take a shower tonight. I go into the bathroom and look at the bathtub:

No way am I getting in there. I have seen *Psycho* multiple times and I am not going to run the risk that I will be standing behind that shower curtain, naked and unarmed, when an evil entity bursts in and stabs me to death or—worse— tosses a lobster at me. I decide to shower in the morning.

I place my wallet and keys on the dresser, plug my phone into the charger, undress, get into bed and, lulled by the gentle 140 mph breeze from the window air conditioner thirty inches from my head, quickly fall into a deep sleep.

I wake early the next morning, feeling refreshed. I get out of bed, stretch and glance over toward the dresser. Suddenly, I notice something: *My wallet and keys are exactly where I left them.* So either the spirits decided not to move them or— we cannot rule this out—they moved them *and then moved them back.*

Either way, they have toyed with me enough. I shower quickly in the Death Tub, dress, pack, check out and get into my rental car. At this hour, Cassadaga is even quieter than usual. There's not a living soul around.

And then, as I drive away from the hotel through the empty streets, it happens: I hear a voice. I swear this is the truth. The voice is speaking directly to me, guiding me. It is telling me to proceed on the path that I am on and then, in 1.5 miles, to turn left.

I obey the voice, because it's coming from the GPS. I do not understand how it works, but I believe in it. It gets me out of Cassadaga.

I don't mean to knock Cassadaga: It's a nice, creepy little town. If that's what you're looking for, by all means you should visit, maybe spend a night at the Cassadaga Hotel. Ask for Room 2: It's windy, but the spirits are reasonable. Be sure to say hi to my mom.

# THE VILLAGES

I'm driving north on the Florida Turnpike on a quest to find the Fountain of Youth.

Not literally, of course. The Fountain of Youth is purely mythical, like the Easter Bunny, or edible vegan food. My destination is a real place, a place where—if the stories are true—you can lead a wild, carefree and passionate lifestyle, possibly involving sex, *even if you are a really, really old person*, defined as "a person my age."

What is this place? It's called The Villages. It's the world's largest retirement community and the fastest-growing city in the United States; it now has 115,000 residents, more than double what it had in 2010.

The Villages has received a lot of publicity in recent years because of the supposed wild swinging lifestyles led by some residents. Here, for example, is the headline of a *Daily Mail* story written after a widely publicized 2014 incident in which a sixty-eight-year-old married woman resident of The Villages was caught having sex in one of the community's public squares with a forty-nine-year-old man who was not, if you want to get technical, her husband:

*Ten women to every man, a black market in Viagra, and a "thriving swingers scene": Welcome to The Villages, Florida, where the elderly residents down Sex on the Square cocktail in "honor" of woman, 68, arrested for public sex with toyboy*

Around the same time BuzzFeed ran a feature about The Villages, calling it "a notorious boomtown for boomers who want to spend their golden years with access to 11 a.m. happy hours, thousands of activities, and no-strings-attached sex."

Just about every feature story written about The Villages sooner or later—usually sooner—brings up sex, Viagra and the alleged increase in STDs among the residents. Writers, especially younger writers, tend to get freaked out by the concept of *old people doing it.*

The legend of wild times at The Villages got started with the 2008 book *Leisureville* by Andrew Blechman. It's actually a well-researched, serious work that raises important issues involving aging, retirement and the concept of communities that don't allow children to be residents. But what everybody remembers about *Leisureville* is a chapter about the sexual exploits of a retired biology teacher known as Mr. Midnight, which is the nickname he gave to his penis.

In the book, Mr. Midnight (the man, not the penis) is quoted as saying: "What you've got to understand is that there are at least ten women here to every guy. And they're all hot and horny. It's wonderful."

Far be it from me to correct a former biology teacher, but it turns out that Mr. Midnight's gender ratio for The Villages is a bit off: It's more like ten women to every nine guys. As for the abundant availability of sex, I will tell you later what I found out about that. (Spoiler Alert: Nothing.)

But getting back to my quest. To reach The Villages, I get off the turnpike at the Wildwood (Ha!¹) exit, where I stop briefly at the Florida Citrus Center, a store that sells all kinds of things that tourists need, including T-shirts and baby alli-

---

1. The Wildwood exit is five miles past the Okahumpka Service Plaza. Really.

gators. I'm stopping because I want to take a picture of my all-time favorite Florida tourism sign:

How many times have you said to yourself, "I want to buy a gator head, but I also want to buy wind chimes, and *I don't want to make two stops*"? Me, too. That's why I'm glad to know that the Florida Citrus Center is there for me.

I resume driving and soon enter The Villages, where if you tried to put up a sign like the one at the Florida Citrus Center, you would be executed without trial by officers of the Homeowners Association. The Villages—which covers thirty-two square miles spread over three counties—is very, very orderly. The houses are all one-story, all colored some shade of light beige or light gray and all subject to many strict rules regarding decorations and landscaping. The houses are set close together on a vast network of streets with the kinds of made-up names that people come up with when they're writing bad novels or need a bunch of street names in a hurry— Barksdale Drive, Intrepid Terrace, Paisley Way, Nautilus Lane, Whisper Street, etc.

Everything—the houses, the yards, the streets, the sidewalks—is uniform in appearance and well maintained. There's no litter, no graffiti, no commercial signs, no sketchy individuals walking around. In fact, there's not a lot of walking: Most people are driving, and many of them are driving golf carts. The Villages has more than sixty thousand golf carts; there are special roads, tunnels and service stations for them, and many residents use them almost exclusively to get around. They *love* their golf carts, in The Villages; people

spend thousands and thousands of dollars customizing them. In The Villages, your golf cart, unlike your house, can reflect the real, unique *you*.

I arrive at my hotel, the Waterfront Inn, which is in Lake Sumter Landing, one of The Villages' three commercial areas or "Town Squares." There are some people checking out a charity Christmas decoration auction in the lobby. Nobody appears to be having sex.

I check in, then head back out, driving to another Town Square, called Spanish Springs, which has a Spanish architectural theme. Each of the squares has a theme, kind of like Disney's Tomorrowland, Fantasyland, Frontierland, etc., ex-

*Fake historic plaque.*

cept instead of rides there are stores and restaurants. The buildings were all built recently, but in pretend old-fashioned style. Weirdly—at least, I find it weird—many of them have "historic plaques" out front on which are written elaborate, made-up histories about the made-up people who lived in this building decades ago, when neither the building nor the town existed.

Don't get me wrong: Spanish Springs is nice. But it's nice in the way Disney's Main Street, U.S.A., is nice. Nice, but fake.

Standing in a fountain next to the square is a statue of the Founding Father of The Villages, Harold Schwartz.

Schwartz began what ultimately became The Villages as a mobile-home park in the 1970s. It was a modest endeavor until the early 1980s, when Schwartz brought in his son,

H. Gary Morse, an advertising executive; together, they began to create a new kind of development. Instead of selling mobile-home lots, they started building an entire community—not just homes, but also stores, restaurants, swimming pools and golf courses. Many golf courses. They sold a lifestyle to retirees, and it was a *nice* lifestyle, safe and convenient and fun, and people loved it. The Villages grew like crazy, becoming increasingly upscale; the Schwartz/Morse family became very, very rich.

Both Schwartz and Morse have died, but the family—people capitalize it, The Family—still tightly controls The Villages and still owns just about everything except the private homes. Critics of The Family see it as secretive and sinister, but most residents of The Villages seem pretty happy with the way things run.

Every night, in all three of the Town Squares, there is live music. People come to listen, dance and—this is one area in which The Villages is far superior to Disney—drink alcoholic beverages sold from booths at reasonable prices. When I arrive in Spanish Springs, some older musicians (defined as "musicians who are probably younger than I am") are setting up on a bandstand. They're called the Caribbean Chillers and they go on at 5. It's a cool night, but already a nice crowd is gathering, a couple hundred people. They're taking green plastic chairs from stacks and arranging them around the bandstand. This is a nightly ritual.

I head to an alcohol booth—I'm the only customer—and order a glass of wine. The bartender looks at his watch and tells me that the two-for-one happy hour starts in twelve minutes, at 5 p.m.

"Is that what everybody's waiting for?" I ask.

"They always do," he says.

I tell him I want to start being happy now, so I pay $5 and he pours a generous amount of wine into a plastic cup. I sip my wine and study the crowd. It's mostly couples, dressed casually; almost everybody's wearing shorts or jeans, sneakers or sandals. Most of them are sitting on their green plastic chairs, patiently waiting for the music to start. Nobody appears to be having sex. Maybe they do that during happy hour.

At 5 p.m. sharp, the Caribbean Chillers, who are basically a Jimmy Buffett clone band, launch into their first song, a mellow country tune. There's not much reaction from the crowd. That changes on the second song, which, you will be shocked to learn, is "Margaritaville." Immediately, people are up and dancing.

It turns out that residents of The Villages really like to dance. It's like being at a wedding or bar mitzvah when the DJ puts on some ancient Boomer favorite like "Sweet Home

Alabama" and all the older people, all the aunts and uncles, swarm the floor and start lurching around while the young people watch from the sidelines and snicker. Except that here in The Villages, there are no young people, and nobody is snickering. Nobody here cares at *all* how you dance. This is one of the nicest things about The Villages.

The predominant style of dancing is what I would describe as "White Person." There are three main types of White Person dancers:

1. **People performing random freestyle moves such as you would have seen in a disco in 1973.** This is how I dance.[2] You see some of this at The Villages, but you see more of the other two types.

2. **Couples who took dance lessons and are faithfully executing the steps they learned.** These couples tend to dance with serious expressions, as if they are carrying out a set of instructions required to complete a two-person task, such as installing drapes.

3. **Line dancers.** This is by far the largest group. Line dancing is big in The Villages. And I'm not just talk-

2. Yes, I am a white person.

ing about your simple line dances, such as your Electric Slide. I'm talking about elaborate line dances, complex, multi-step routines that you have to practice before you get out there in the mass of people all moving together, frowning, looking down at their feet, as they run through the steps in their heads: ... *two three now rock forward now back now turn two three now kick and left slide two three now* ...

The Caribbean Chillers play some more Jimmy Buffett. More people are arriving on their golf carts and lining up for two-for-one drinks. A lot of people are dancing. I watch an elegant-looking, tastefully dressed woman—I'm guessing late sixties, early seventies—walk up to the bandstand, set her purse down next to it and start dancing. She's a good dancer, fluid and graceful. She does a series of moves from the sixties—the Twist, the Jerk, the Swim—all by herself. The song finishes; she picks up her purse and walks back to her green plastic chair.

It occurs to me, sipping my wine, that back in the late sixties, when I played in a rock band[3] at Haverford College, I

---

3. The Federal Duck.

might have seen this very woman, or some of these other dancers, gyrating in the strobe light as we belted out anthems of youthful rebellion:

*People try to put us d-down / Just because we get around...*

Maybe long ago, behind some gym or fraternity house when my band was taking a break, I even shared a joint with some of these people. And now here we are, nearly fifty years later, talkin' 'bout my generation, drinking reasonably priced wine and getting around in golf carts.

At least we're still dancing.

The Caribbean Chillers finish another song. The lead singer says, "We're rockin' right here, Spanish Springs." Then the band kicks into "Mustang Sally." This is a great dancing song, and the Caribbean Chillers are nailing it. A large line dance forms in front of the bandstand. But my eye is drawn to one man who is not part of the line; he's all alone in front of the bandstand, where the elegant woman was. He's bald and large. He's wearing a striped shirt tucked into voluminous shorts, held up by suspenders. He's dancing like an absolute wild man, spinning, waving his arms around, doing karate moves and being exuberant and just generally not giving any kind of a shit. He's wonderful. I am falling in love with this man from afar.

*Gary Locks dancing next to, but not with, line dancers.*

The song ends. I head over and introduce myself to the man. He tells me he is Gary Locks and he's a retired lieutenant colonel, United States Air Force. He has also worked in security and for the TSA. He's extremely cheerful. He's seventy-two and married.

"My wife is parking the car," he says.

Locks says he moved to The Villages from Ohio ten months ago and he loves it. "This is Disney World for adults," he says. (Residents of The Villages say this a lot.)

I ask him about his dancing. He says he dances every night. "Since I moved here, I dropped from 270 to 240 pounds."

I ask about the karate moves. "I learned that in the military and security," he says. "Also, Elvis did that. I have incorporated some of his moves."

He says his dancing is popular with the ladies. "They find me, eventually," he says. "I've had girls thirteen to ninety ask me to dance."

I ask about his suspenders. "Women love them," he says. "I've had them unhook 'em."

I offer to buy him a drink, but he shakes his head.

"I've never had a beer or cigarette in my life," he says. "But I've had plenty of guns pointed at me."

His wife, Gayle, joins us. I remark on her husband's dancing.

"I just let him go," she says.

The band starts another song, and Gary Locks, dancing machine, suspendered stud of Spanish Springs, heads back out to resume his rocking retirement.

I get back in my car and drive back to Lake Sumter Landing to check out the nightlife there. En route, I listen to WVLG, the AM radio station owned and operated by The Family. They also operate a TV channel and publish a daily newspaper, *The Villages Daily Sun*, that's fat with advertising, more prosperous-looking than many big-city newspapers. It carries a respectable amount of national and international news, but it's heaviest on happenings in The Villages—news about clubs (there are seventeen million clubs), golf tournaments, health and fitness, real estate, homeowner associations, decorating, shopping and so on. (The day I arrive, there's an article about a Chick-fil-A franchise celebrating its tenth anniversary in The Villages. "Coleslaw isn't a very popular item on our menu nationally," states the franchise owner, "but it is here.")

The WVLG DJ plays "Runaway" by Del Shannon, followed by "Higher and Higher" by Jackie Wilson. I love both of those songs. I listened to them on AM car radios in the sixties. I roll down the windows and crank up the volume.

I get to Lake Sumter Landing and I immediately realize that it is the place to be, because it is swarming with golf carts. They're parked everywhere, row after row of them.

Eventually, I find a spot for my rental car and walk to the Town Square, where tonight's entertainment is the Paul Vesco Band. They're funkier than the Caribbean Chillers; in fact, when I arrive, they're singing, "Play that funky music white boy." There are two large herds of line dancers here. They're dedicated and focused, and the dances they're doing are even more complex than the ones over in Spanish Springs. They keep it up for several more songs and then the singer announces that they're going to do a slow tune for the couples out there. The band starts playing the Etta James version of "At Last (My Love Has Come Along)." This is a slow, sensuous, achingly soulful song, so naturally the line dancers ... *keep right on line dancing*. Nothing can stop these people from executing their steps. The band could play the *William Tell Overture*, or the Wedding March, and they would line-dance to it. That's how they roll, Villages-style.

Several couples also get up and slow-dance; one couple is dancing while holding their little white dog between them, its head sticking out from between their bellies. It looks ridiculous, but nobody seems to care.

Back where these people came from—Ohio or Minnesota or New York or wherever—they would never dance in public with their dog. In fact, none of these people, these aging Boomers, would be out dancing on a random Thursday night, or pretty much any other night. But here they can dance *every night,* and down a few reasonably priced cocktails if they feel like it, and ride home in their golf cart. They can go golfing the next day, whatever day it is, and then go dancing again the next night, and do this again and again, every day if they want, until they die, which could be any time because nobody's getting any younger, so why not enjoy yourself while you're still around?

I can totally see the appeal.

I watch the dancers for a while, then walk past the vast herd of golf carts en route to my car, which now seems like a totally Squaresville vehicle for me to be driving. I return to the hotel and stick my head into the bar/dining room area, where a few people are having dinner, but nothing else is happening. It occurs to me that I've been here for an entire day and have yet to see anybody having sex. Maybe tomorrow.

The next morning I have breakfast at the Panera's in downtown Lake Sumter. It's busy, every table filled. Breakfast is a social event here. There's free Wi-Fi, but I'm the only person in the entire restaurant using a laptop computer. I see one person looking at her phone. Everybody else is either talking or *reading a newspaper.* It's eerie, like suddenly we're back in 2003.

After breakfast, I stroll around Lake Sumter a bit, listening to the sounds of WVLG playing from speakers mounted on the lampposts. I pass Starbucks, where a group of maybe a dozen crusty old farts—regulars, by the look of them—are having coffee at some outdoor tables, telling jokes and making loud, raucous fun of each other, which they're comfortable doing here because *this is their town.*

I make my way to The Villages Sales and Information Center, which is in a new building pretending that it's an old building that was once a grand hotel. I sign up to take the official one-hour trolley tour of The Villages. There are seventeen of us on the tour, including two British couples and two African-American women, whom I mention because The Villages is 98 percent white; less than 1 percent of the residents are African-American.

We board the trolley and meet our tour guide. Her name is Carol Lynn Olson and she moved here from Ohio. To say she likes The Villages is like saying Romeo liked Juliet. Carol *loves* The Villages, and although she has given many trolley tours before ours, her enthusiasm never wanes, even slightly, during the hour.

"This is not a sales tour," she tells us, the understanding being that The Villages doesn't need to sell itself because so many people want to live here. She says she won't be showing us houses: "In The Villages, it's not about the house. It's about the lifestyle."

She starts by telling us about the ready availability and high quality of medical care here—hospitals, doctors, emergency care. She says that the emergency response time in The Villages is under four minutes, versus ten minutes nationally, and that the heart-attack-survival rate here is over 40 percent, versus 10 percent nationally.

Moving on from survival to leisure, Carol shows us some of the community recreation centers and tells us that currently The Villages has seventy-eight swimming pools, some of which are adults-only. ("If you're like me, you don't always want to listen to somebody else's grandchildren yell 'Marco' / 'Polo' for three hours.") There are twelve country clubs, and golf courses out the wazoo. "One gentleman claims to have played 681 rounds of golf in one year," notes Carol.

One of the people on the tour is a resident of The Villages, a tan, fit-looking guy named Bob, showing around a couple of his buddies visiting from North Dakota. Carol asks Bob to tell the rest of us about his life here. He says he loves it. He plays a lot of golf, he plays pickleball,[4] he plays softball, he's in a convertible club. "I'm just so busy," he says.

---

4. A mutant form of tennis played on a smaller court, popular with seniors.

Carol says that retirees who move here are actually doing their children a favor by removing the burden of worry: "The kids are happy that Mom's not sitting home with nothing to do." She stresses the convenience of being able to get around by golf cart, of having everything she needs right here in The Villages, including big-name entertainment. Among the acts she has seen here are Tony Orlando, Lee Greenwood, Bobby Vinton and Lesley Gore.

"I don't have to go anywhere," she says.

As she talks, we're driving past mile after mile of houses, all one-story, all the same style, all set close together on tidy lots, all colored some variation of beige or light gray. The houses are nice enough, but they blur together into one long beige-ish/gray-ish line, disappearing into the distance.

At one point, Carol touches, obliquely, on the rigid conformity of the architecture, the restrictions on landscaping and decorating. "You can make your home very unique and very personal," she says. She sounds a little defensive.

Carol tells us a little about the history of The Villages. Her tone becomes reverent when she speaks of Founding Father Harold Schwartz: "He was a dreamer. He was a visionary." She says that although Schwartz and his son have died, The Family is still in control: "The dream does go on."

And you can be part of the dream; that's the message. You

don't have to live in a hectic and disorganized and scary world that has little time for or interest in older people like you. You can come live in this safe orderly place and putt around on your custom golf cart and do pretty much whatever you want, and nobody will judge you, because this whole place is *about* you—not your kids, not future generations, not society in general: *You*. You've worked hard, you've sacrificed enough. Now it's pickleball time, dammit.

That's the message.

The tour ends. Carol, noting that she is being politically incorrect, wishes us a Merry Christmas. Some of the people on the tour go into the sales office to talk about houses. I head back out onto the pretend historic streets of Lake Sumter, where I encounter the two African-American women who were on the tour, and we get to chatting. They're cousins.

One of them, Ora Hardy, is a retired court reporter from the Chicago area; she's sixty-six and looking for a warm place to settle down. She's planning to rent a place in The Villages for a while to see how she likes it.

"I'm an older lady with a dog," she says. "I want to be someplace where I can have a sense of safety, not have to worry about looking around."

So she likes the security of The Villages. But she's not sold yet. "I have real reservations about the lack of diversity." She says there's a "manufactured sweetness" about the way people treat her here, though she notes that this is "something that you're used to when you're sixty-six."

I tell her that if she truly wants to experience the overpowering whiteness of The Villages, she needs to check out the line dancing. She and her cousin laugh. I wish her luck and we part company. I head back toward my hotel, crossing the Lake Sumter square, which is deserted. The WVLG lamppost speakers are playing "Cool Jerk."

In the afternoon I drive over to Paddock Square, the newest of the Town Squares, which has a fake historic western motif. There are big doin's here today: They're lighting the Christmas tree and there's a bunch of entertainment scheduled. The festivities start at 4, but at 2:30, when I arrive, the square and bleachers are already filling up. Soon, the whole place is full, and lines are forming at the beverage booths. This is the place to be at The Villages today.

At 4 sharp, the first act goes on. These are the Silver Rockettes, a group of ladies wearing Santa Claus capes and hats over their black-and-silver costumes. They march to the square in unison, with their hands on their hips in a certain way that has no doubt been perfected during rehearsals in a recreation center. It's a truly wonderful look.

The Silver Rockettes get a nice hand from the crowd as they launch into their dance routine, "Here Comes Santa Claus," the Elvis Presley version. Their choreography is patterned after the famous Radio City Music Hall Rockettes except that instead of high kicks and other fast-paced precision dance moves, the Silver Rockettes confine themselves to small, cautious steps, hand gestures and coordinated head nods. This results in the following discussion between two women near me:

FIRST WOMAN: Why aren't they kicking?

SECOND WOMAN: Women of our age can't kick very high.

FIRST WOMAN: Wanna bet? I'm eighty-six.

The Silver Rockettes finish "Here Comes Santa Claus" and remove their capes for their next number, "Let It Snow," which they perform seated on a row of chairs. Here, in addition to the synchronized head nods and hand gestures, they are able to raise their feet in the air. This gets a nice hand from the crowd, but it does not impress my neighbor, the first woman, who says: "That was it? Sitting-down kicking?"

When the Silver Rockettes finish, they take a bow, don their Santa hats and capes and walk off with their hands on their hips in a certain practiced way.

Next up on the stage is Scooter the DJ, a regular in The Villages, with a good, wiseacre delivery, comical props and a stream of well-practiced jokes about subjects such as the dangers of dancing with a hip replacement. The crowd loves Scooter; he immediately gets people up and dancing. Pretty soon he has a huge crowd, including Santa and Mrs. Claus, out there doing—prepare to not be surprised—the Electric Slide.

As I'm watching this, I'm thinking two things:

1. This has to the whitest, squarest thing happening anywhere in America.
2. These people are *really* enjoying themselves.

The Electric Slide ends and Scooter gets the crowd doing— of course!—the "Y.M.C.A." dance. The whole downtown area is now jammed; the lines are long at the beverage booths. Scooter announces the next act, which is the Gemstone Dancers, a group of gals in semi-western attire who perform country-style line dances.

I decide it's time to mosey back to Lake Sumter, where I have dinner at a restaurant called City Fire. I eat at the bar and get into a conversation with the couple sitting next to me. The woman is named Debra Barran; she's sixty-three and she loves The Villages. "On the one hand," she says, "it's a place where there's a lot of older people. But the other side of the coin is, they *appreciate* older people."

Her companion, who identifies himself only as Len and

gives his age, unconvincingly, as thirty-nine, also loves The Villages. "This is the best place in the world," he says. Debra nods.

I head back to my hotel. Tonight there's dancing in the bar. A DJ named Pat Atkinson is playing excellent music, killer dance songs like Marcia Ball's "A Fool in Love."[5] The crowd is about fifty-fifty men/women and many of them are very good dancers, obviously regulars here. At one point, they perform a line dance, but it actually looks pretty cool, for a line dance.

I drink a couple of beers and watch the crowd. I figure that if there really is a wild sex scene going on in The Villages, there should be some kind of hot pickup action happening at this bar. But all I see is dancing. Maybe they're waiting for me to leave before they start having wild sex. I head for bed.

The next morning, I take one last stroll over to the Lake Sumter Square, where the Florida Lottery is holding a big daylong event consisting of various lottery promotions, including a chance to win a golf cart. There are a bunch of booths, a prize wheel, and tables stacked with T-shirts, water

---

5. If you don't know it, stop reading this and go listen to that song *right now.*

bottles and other cheap giveaway items. It's only 9 and the event doesn't start until 10, but already at least a hundred people have gathered. They're sitting in plastic chairs, watching the lottery people set up. Over the lamppost speakers WVLG is playing "Double Shot (Of My Baby's Love)" by the Swingin' Medallions.

I check out of my hotel and head back to Miami, the disorderly, haphazard, weird, sensuous, sometimes dangerous, often insane and always unpredictable place where I live. I'm happy to get home. I like having a certain amount of disorder in my life, and I like living in a blue house. I couldn't live in The Villages: To me, it feels too much like a giant line dance, everybody following the same steps.

But I'm not knocking the people who love The Villages. As an aging Boomer, I'm not about to criticize people of my generation who want to spend whatever time they have left doing whatever they really want to do in the company of people who don't view them as fossils. And if they really are having wild sex up there, I say more power to them. It's *good* for people our age to have sex. It upsets the children.

# GATORLAND

Today I'm visiting Gatorland, which proudly bills itself as "The Alligator Capital of the World," as well as, more modestly, "Orlando's Best Half Day Attraction." This is the place to go if you want to observe alligators going about their normal daily alligator routine of not moving for hours on end. Also, if you have a problem alligator that has been a nuisance in your neighborhood, on your golf course, in your Jacuzzi, etc., Gatorland will take it off your hands. It is a haven for troubled alligators. It also has crocodiles, which are also motionless but can be distinguished from alligators by the biological fact that the sign on their pen says CROCODILES.

Gatorland is located on the Orange Blossom Trail, just up the road a piece[1] from Tupperware world headquarters.[2] It's a family-owned business that has been around since 1949, way before Disney. It's proud of its Old Florida heritage, and it has a laid-back, non-slick, this-ain't-the-Magic-Kingdom, redneck-y vibe. For example, the gift shop sells flasks. Also, there are a lot of jokey signs like this:

When you enter Gatorland, the first wildlife you see is— Spoiler Alert—alligators. A *buttload* of alligators, dozens and dozens of them on wooden platforms surrounded by water. They are sprawled haphazardly, often on top of each other, as if they're having a wild reptile orgy, except that they are not

---

1. One piece = .7 miles.

2. This is where, in 1987, backed by three other professional newspaper journalists, I performed "The Tupperware Blues" in front of a thousand Tupperware distributors. You missed it.

moving. Some of them look like they have not moved since the Reagan administration. It's like the Department of Motor Vehicles, but with alligators.

Every once in a while, an alligator gets a bee in its bonnet and *verrrry* slowly moves forward maybe three inches. Then, not wanting to be branded as too much of a go-getter by the others, it resumes being motionless.

While strolling on the boardwalk over the alligator ponds, I come across a Mold-A-Matic machine that will make you a souvenir alligator toy right on the spot in just thirty seconds, except that the machine, in keeping with long-standing Mold-A-Matic tradition, is out of order.

Seeking action, or at least movement, I head over to Panther Springs, which features two endangered Florida panthers, Neiko and Lucy, brother and sister, who were born in a rescue center and, according to a sign, "brought to their gorgeous new home at Gatorland to help educate our visitors on the peril of the Florida panther." They're in a large landscaped enclosure with a glass wall on one side. One of them—Lucy, I believe—is sleeping under a bench, but Neiko is doing slow circuits of the perimeter, prowling around and around and around and around and around and around and around, looking for a way out that is never there no matter how many times he goes around and around and around. Each time he passes the glass wall, his powerful body just inches from tourists taking pictures of him, I get the feeling that he's thinking some panther version of *If I could just get through this invisible thing, I would definitely educate these visitors.*

*Neiko looking through the glass.*

Leaving Panther Springs, I check out the pythons, who are motionless, as are the giant tortoises, and The Snakes of Florida, and the rare white alligators, and the various other specialty and/or celebrity alligators, all of them exhibiting the same level of activity as a fire hydrant.

One of the celebrity gators is named Chester. The sign on his pen says:

**"CHESTER" The Big Dog Eater!**

This big fellar's name is Chester and he loved eating dogs in Tampa, FL. At 13½ feet long and 1,000 pounds, he could put away some "hounds." We saved him from trappers who wanted to make a suitcase out of him. He don't get along real well with other gators so he gets this cool bachelor pad with private pool.

Chester is lying motionless in his pool, staring ahead with a stoic expression, perhaps dreaming of the days when he roamed free in Tampa, chowing down on Labradoodles.

Near Chester is an exhibit of parrots, who, to their credit, sometimes turn their heads. Also there's a petting zoo—excuse me, *pettin'* zoo—where one of the posted rules is NO EATING THE ANIMAL FOOD.

A little past that is the Upclose Encounters outdoor theater, where several times a day wisecracking Gatorland guys put on a comical show in which they display venomous snakes and freak people out by such antics as putting tarantulas on their heads. For the grand finale they have some tourists stand in a line, facing the audience and holding out their arms, with orders not to turn around. Then from backstage the Gatorland guys bring out, and swiftly drape across the victims' outstretched arms, a ten-foot tapeworm.

Not really, although that would make for a truly entertaining Upclose Encounter. What the guys place on the tourists' arms is an albino Burmese python, which the tourists hold nervously while the Gatorland guys make wisecracks about being swallowed.

The Burmese python is the brand of snake that is taking over the Everglades by eating all the other animals. This has led to the creation of one of my favorite Florida government programs: The Python Challenge. This is a contest run by the Florida Fish and Wildlife Conservation Commission, which invites the public to hunt pythons and offers cash prizes to whoever brings in the most pythons, or the longest python, dead or alive. Basically, the theme is: *Florida—Come kill our snakes!*

I think this is a great way to remove pests, and would like to see Florida adapt the concept to other invasive species, such as New York Jets fans. I'm not suggesting that we *kill* them, of course. I'm suggesting that we trap them humanely, put them in trucks and release them back in New York. If they come back, *then* we should kill them.[3]

As I leave the Upclose Encounters show, I have an exciting upclose encounter of my own when I behold a sight I never expected to see in my lifetime—a sight so unlikely, so implausible, so *impossible*, that I almost question my own senses. I blink several times, but it's still there, incredible as it seems, right in front of my eyes: *a Mold-A-Matic machine without an out-of-order sign apologizing for the inconvenience.* MAKE YOUR OWN GATORLAND WRESTLER, it says.

I approach the Mold-A-Matic cautiously, fearful that I will spook it into suddenly being out of order. Carefully I insert two dollar bills. I watch in amazement as the Mold-A-Matic wheezes and whirs, then produces the toy, which is a replica,

---

3. I am kidding, of course. Only if they come back a second time should we kill them.

made of what appears to be radioactive mucus, of a hat-wearing man who appears to be having sex with an alligator.

As I am photographing the toy, a father and his young daughter stop to look at the Mold-A-Matic. I hand the girl the toy, which is still warm, and tell her she can have it. She is delighted. The father thanks me, though he seems less enthusiastic.

My next stop is the Gator Wrestlin' Show. A big crowd has gathered, sitting on bleachers around a sandpit surrounded by water containing several dozen motionless alligators, every single one of which is thinking: *Please, please, PLEASE don't pick me.*

The show, like Upclose Encounters, features two wise-cracking Gatorland guys. After some introductory wisecracks, they have a member of the audience select an alligator. One of the guys grabs this gator—which is thinking: *NOOOOOO*—by the tail and drags it onto the sand, where he commences wrestlin' it, by which I mean sitting on it. I have seen alligator "wrestling" many times, and I have never seen an alligator make even the slightest effort to resist. The gators display the same fighting spirit as a Barcalounger.

The Gatorland guy keeps up a stream of comical patter while performing the standard gator-wrestling maneuvers, including prying the gator's mouth open. For his grand finale, he holds the gator's mouth open with his chin while everybody takes pictures. The gator submits to all of this sto-

ically, although it is clearly thinking: *Why? In the name of God, WHY?*

From the Gator Wrestlin' venue, I head over to Pearl's Smokehouse for lunch. While waiting in line, I study the menu; the most expensive item, at $10.49, is the Gator Nuggets. That's right: In addition to rescuing alligators, Gatorland serves them deep-fried. It is a full-service gator facility.

I decide to try the nuggets. Apparently, I'm the only one ordering them; the cashier says they'll take a few minutes. But it's worth the wait when the nuggets arrive piping hot from the fryer with a festive presentation featuring toothpicks.

I select a nugget and take a small bite, which I am able to successfully swallow after approximately forty-five minutes of chewing. I honestly think it would be easier to eat the Mold-A-Matic toy. I decide to pass on the remainder of the nuggets. My hat is off to whatever kind of animal is able to eat alligators in the wild, uncooked.

I head back toward the entrance of the park, because it's almost time for the signature event at Gatorland, a show that, in my opinion, is one of the best things[4] you will find at any attraction in Florida or the world in general: the legendary Gator Jumparoo.

---

4. No, I am not being sarcastic.

A big crowd has gathered around the Jumparoo pond for the show, which stars two Gatorland guys pretending to be subliterate overalls-wearing hillbillies named Bubba and Cooter. After some comical preliminary hijinks establishing that they have the IQs of yogurt, Bubba and Cooter get down to the heart of the Jumparoo, which is going out on a platform and dangling chicken carcasses over the water. This, at last, is something that the alligators consider worth moving for. They swarm toward the platform and lunge out of the water, snapping their jaws.

The tourists, who have been divided into Team Bubba and Team Cooter, cheer when one of the gators on their side snags a chicken carcass and gulps it down. I'm on Team Bubba and I am definitely cheering. I find the Gator Jumparoo to be a lot more exciting than, for example, professional baseball.

The show ends and I head for the exit, because I know nothing will surpass the Jumparoo. It has been an enjoyable half day for me, except for the Nugget Encounter. Gatorland has a lot to see, even if most of it doesn't move, and I like the fact they don't take themselves too seriously. Also they get major bonus points for having a working Mold-A-Matic, which is ironic because it results in my decision to award Gatorland, using the Florida Tourist Attraction Rating System, 4 out of a possible 5 out-of-order Mold-A-Matics.

I get into my car and exit the parking lot, looking for a place to eat. I'm starving and I know exactly what I want to have for lunch.

Chicken.

# LOCK & LOAD
## MIAMI

There comes a time in a man's life when a man must man up and be a man by summoning up his manhood and doing something manly. For me, that time is today. And the place is Lock & Load Miami.

Lock & Load is a shooting range that offers a "Machine Gun Experience": You pay them money and they let you shoot actual machine guns emitting actual bullets. The Lock & Load website boasts that they offer "the nation's greatest variety of fully automatic firearms with over 25 fully automatic machine guns available for use in packages and a la carte." The packages include the 007, the Special Forces Eastern Bloc, the Special Forces Israel (which includes an Uzi), the

Boss (a.k.a. "El Jefe"), the Scarface and others. For enhanced manliness, you can augment your package with handguns.

I am here with my friend and cousin-in-law Ron Ungerman, who is visiting Miami with his wife, Sonia. They originally had other plans for today, probably shopping, but when I asked Ron if he wanted to go shoot machine guns instead, he responded, quote, "Fuck yes."

Sonia was less excited about it, as was my wife, Michelle. I am a huge fan of females as a gender, but they tend to display a baffling lack of enthusiasm for violent destruction. Show me a group of individuals who are spending a Sunday afternoon entertaining themselves by using explosives to blow up, say, major appliances, and I will show you a group of males. Any females in the area will be holding their fingers in their ears and saying, *"Why?"*

That was how our wives felt about the Machine Gun Experience. I tried to discuss my shooting-package options with Michelle ahead of time, and it went like this:

> ME (*looking at the Lock & Load website*): Whoa. You can shoot a .50 caliber!
>
> MICHELLE: They just give you a machine gun and let you shoot it?
>
> ME: That's a really big caliber.

MICHELLE: What if you shoot somebody?

ME: Would you think less of me if I didn't get a .50
caliber package?

MICHELLE: What if somebody shoots you?

But, as I say, a man has to do what a man has to do, and so, on this Tuesday morning, Ron and I, without our wives, pull into the parking lot of the Lock & Load building. It's located in Miami's Wynwood District, an area that used to be seedy and crime-ridden but has been gentrified and hipsterfied to the point where the biggest danger today is that you might accidentally purchase non-artisanal food.

The Lock & Load building is painted gunmetal gray and decorated with silhouettes of people holding guns. Next to the entrance, as a fun decorative accessory, is a missile.

Inside, Lock & Load is more inviting—bright, spacious, cheerful and modern, with lots of tables and chairs. It looks kind of like a restaurant, except that the menus on the tables explain the shooting package options and there are machine guns mounted on the wall.

We're greeted by an attractive young woman Sales Associate in a Lock & Load T-shirt. She explains the menu and says we can check out the guns on the wall, if we want, because they've been modified so they can't fire. She leaves, telling us she'll be back to take our order. As we ponder the menu, I overhear the conversation at a nearby table, where a father and his two teenage kids are discussing their package options with another attractive young female Sales Associate.

"I would stay away from the Eastern Bloc," she is telling them. After some mulling, Ron and I make our decisions. He's going with the $179 Scarface package, and I'm going with the $209 Special Forces package. The packages involve different weapons, but in both cases you shoot four different machine guns, twenty-five rounds each. (*Round* is a manly word for "bullet.") Ron and I both add handguns to our packages, at $29 each. Ron selects the Baretta. I go with the Glock, not because I know anything about handguns but because my daughter, Sophie, and I have a running joke about the lyrics to a song called "679" by a hip-hop recording artist[1] named Fetty Wap, who at one point says, "I got a Glock in my 'rari," meaning he has a Glock in his Ferrari. Sophie and I like to indicate how "street" we are by sporadically declaring that we have Glocks in our 'raris. I will never own a 'rari, but I'm thinking it might be fun to say I actually fired a Glock.

The Sales Associate comes back and takes our order, then tells us it will take about ten minutes to load our packages. Ron and I pass the time by photographing each other posing with some of the deactivated wall-mounted weapons. Neither one of us has ever fired a machine gun before, but as soon as we pick up these superbly engineered firearms, feeling their heft as we cradle them in our arms, we undergo a subtle change—a transformation, if you will—from a cou-

---

1. So to speak.

ple of ordinary, non-threatening civilian guys into a pair of world-class douchenozzles.

If Ron and I were ever to, God forbid, find ourselves holding machine guns in actual combat, our only hope of survival would be that the enemy was laughing too hard to aim properly.

Finally, it's time for us to shoot. I'm starting to feel quite nervous. As you have probably gathered, I know basically nothing about guns. I've never owned one, unless you count the Daisy BB gun I had when I was a kid, which—although it could put out somebody's eye, as my mother reminded me repeatedly—was not a lethal weapon. I know this because

I shot my brother Phil with it at fairly close range and he did not die. In my defense, I had a good reason for shooting Phil; namely, I wanted to find out what happens if you shoot somebody with a BB gun. (Answer: He tells your mother.) But mainly I used my BB gun for target practice, by which I mean shooting out every streetlight in the greater Armonk, N.Y., metropolitan area.[2]

In other words, I have not had any meaningful experience with real firearms in my entire life. And now, as Ron and I head toward the firing range, my excitement about shooting machine guns is turning into nervousness and fears of inadequacy. These fears do not subside when we meet our Firearms Specialist, Nick Gulla. He is a tall, trim, sinewy man with a full beard, a deep voice and a handshake that would crush a coconut. He could be a testosterone donor. He is wearing a camo-patterned ball cap, a red Lock & Load polo shirt, tan military-style pants and a sidearm. He makes me feel like I'm wearing a tutu.

Before we go into the shooting range, Nick goes over some basic firearm-handling rules with us, the main ones being (1) always treat the gun as if it's loaded, even if you think it's not;

2. Yes, that was me, and I sincerely apologize, now that the Statute of Limitations has expired.

(2) don't put your finger on the trigger until it's time to shoot; and (3) try not to poop your drawers when the gun goes off. (Nick leaves Rule 3 unspoken, but I definitely hear it.)

Nick then has us hold a dummy machine gun and practice our shooting stance. You're supposed to lean pretty far forward to counteract the gun's recoil, which Nick simulates by hitting the muzzle of the gun with the palm of his hand. Both Ron and I have trouble with the stance; we tend to topple forward, which of course would violate another important rule: *Do not fall down while shooting a gun.*

Eventually, with Nick's patient help, Ron and I master the art of standing up. Nick gives us safety glasses and ear protectors and we go into the shooting range. There's a line of shooting positions separated by steel dividers. Suspended in a wire frame in front of each shooting position, maybe twenty-five feet away, is a paper target displaying the shape of a male torso from the waist up.

The target has no facial features, but I like to imagine that he's the guy—let's call him Doug—who always sits near me in airports and has many important calls to make on his mobile phone. Somehow Doug has not yet figured out—despite the fact that we have had mobile phones for decades—that the people on the other end can hear normal conversational speech so THERE IS NO NEED TO TALK LOUD. Doug communicates at the same decibel level as a leaf blower. It does not trouble him, if he is even aware of it, that everybody around him hates him more than Hitler, who, for all his flaws, is at least dead.

Am I saying that I would like to shoot Doug in the head with a machine gun just for talking loud on his phone? Of course not! I would like to shoot Doug in his center mass, which is represented on the target by a red oval in the middle of Doug's chest. This is what you're supposed to aim for.

Ron and I take turns shooting. The procedure is, Nick tells the shooter a little about the gun, then shows him how to load and fire it. When the shooter is shooting, Nick always stands very close behind him, almost touching him, presumably so that if the shooter were to try to do anything stupid, such as turn around, Nick could take corrective action in the form of breaking the shooter's spine like an Olive Garden breadstick.

Neither Ron nor I do anything stupid, which is a miracle because at this point both of us (we discussed this later) have so much adrenaline swirling around inside us that we have the functional IQs of cantaloupes. When Nick explains a gun to me, I'm nodding thoughtfully, but my brain is screaming, *OHMIGOD I'M ABOUT TO SHOOT A MACHINE GUN OHMIGOD I'M ABOUT TO SHOOT A MACHINE GUN OHMIGOD I'M . . .* and so on. The result is, I'm hearing Nick's voice, but I'm not really understanding what he's saying. To me, it sounds like this:

> NICK (*displaying gun*): OK, this is a Wacklestein-Frampler X-839 fully automatic strategic tactical death carbine, which is used by law enforcement, Coast Guard canine units and Special Delta Attack Squadron Forces in SWAT raids, cliff assaults, field exorcisms and anti-submarine operations. It shoots four million rounds per second and has a range of seventeen miles. You load the magazine here, then all you do is pull this lever back, turn this knob a quarter turn counterclockwise and slide this switch to the second notch while pressing this button and engaging this mechanism here, making sure

you line up this triangle with the red circle
and keep these two dots in the center of the
hypotenuse and whatever you do don't glog the
fedelwink. Got it?

ME: *Nodding.*

MY BRAIN: OHMIGOD I'M ABOUT TO SHOOT
A MACHINE GUN.

So when Nick hands me the machine gun, he has to slowly
re-explain everything. Finally, I get the gun loaded, and I'm
ready. I assume the stance and take the safety off. I aim
as best I can at Doug's center mass. Then I squeeze the trigger and

*HO.*

*LY.*

*SHIT.*

First of all, it's loud, even with the ear protection. Also,
there's flame and smoke coming out of the muzzle and shell
casings flying everywhere. Also the gun is jumping around in
my hands. I have no idea where the bullets are going. Fortunately, there are only twenty-five of them, and they're coming
out superfast—*BANG BANG BANG BANG*—so it's over in
about two seconds.

With shaking hands, I set the gun down. I look at Doug.

I did not get every round into his center mass. Some of my rounds may have ended up in Venezuela. But Doug is definitely, as Fetty Wap would say, "iced."

I finish off Doug—you can't be too careful—a total of five times, four times with machine guns and once with a Glock. One of the machine guns is an HK416, which is rumored to be the gun that Navy SEAL Team 6 used to take out Osama bin Laden. It is a badass weapon, and as an American I am proud to say it was part of my package.

When Ron and I are done shooting, we're both totally wired, like squirrels on speed. We are giddy and euphoric. We agree that the Machine Gun Experience is one of the

most fun and exciting things we have ever done, which is all the more impressive when you consider that we have both had sex, although not with each other.

Nick asks us if we want to keep our targets, and we're all HELL YES we want to keep our targets. Doug is currently hanging on a wall in my home office, where he serves as a sobering reminder of what one lone citizen is capable of doing with a machine gun to a sheet of unarmed paper hanging approximately twenty-five feet away.

The only way I can think of to improve the Machine Gun Experience would be if you could select your own target. Imagine how enjoyable it would be to fire a burst of twenty-five rounds into, for example, the U.S. Tax code, or a low-flow toilet, or a fruitcake, or a big-screen TV showing an episode of *Keeping Up With the Kardashians*.

But let us not quibble. The Machine Gun Experience is magnificent the way it is, which is why I am awarding it an unprecedented 6 out of a possible 5 out-of-order Mold-A-Matic machines.

I am definitely going back to Lock & Load. And, next time, I just might choose a package that includes the Barrett M95 sniper rifle, which fires a .50 caliber bullet roughly the size of a Toyota Corolla. Of course I'll have to visualize a different target, since I have already dispatched Doug. I'm thinking this time it will be the Geico Gecko. He will never see it coming.

LIV

It's midnight Saturday on Miami Beach, and I'm with my wife, Michelle, in the lobby of the iconic Fontainebleau Hotel, along with several hundred other people who are hoping to get into LIV.

If you have never heard of LIV, you are, no offense, either a loser or an old person, because LIV is the hottest nightclub on the Beach, which makes it one of the hottest nightclubs in the world. If you don't believe me, ask the Internet, where you'll find LIV on many hottest-club lists. For example, here's what *DJ Mag* (djmag.com) had to say about LIV in its 2015 list of the top 100 clubs:

*Walk past the Bugattis parked out front, through the glass sliding doors and veer right across the marble-floored lobby of Miami's Fontainebleau hotel, and—viola!—you're there. Welcome to chic, celebrity-infested LIV.*

Not to quibble, but: It is, in fact, highly unlikely that you will encounter an actual *viola* inside LIV. What you *will* encounter is a huge—eighteen thousand square feet—lavishly decorated space with a big dance floor and flashing laser lights and a nuclear sound system. There are bars selling $20 cocktails, and reserved tables where you can sit if you get "bottle service," which means you pay several hundred dollars and up—sometimes way up—for a bottle of booze that would cost less than a tenth as much at a liquor store. Also there are private skyboxes, which will cost you even more. People routinely spend thousands—sometimes many thousands—of dollars for an evening at LIV. And usually there's a crowd of people outside beseeching the doormen to allow them to pay the cover charge—$40 and up, depending on the night—so they, too, can go inside and purchase alcohol at high prices.

Why are people clamoring to get into LIV? There are three main reasons:

1. Other people are clamoring to get into LIV.

2. You might see a celebrity or a pro athlete in there. You probably won't. But you *might*.

3. LIV features popular DJs playing recorded music. (As opposed to, God forbid, *unpopular* DJs playing recorded music.)

If you're a guy, there's a fourth reason you're clamoring to get into LIV: The crowd generally contains a high percentage of attractive ladies. The doormen make sure of this. Women, if the doormen deem them hot, will generally get in quickly. Men, especially if there are no women accompanying them, often have to wait longer, and sometimes don't get in at all.

This means that the Fontainebleau lobby, on this Saturday midnight, is a festival of insecurity, kind of like the worst part of high school, except that instead of *Will I get a date for the prom?* the question is *Am I going to get picked by the doorman?* The crowd is mostly people in their twenties—the men in nice jeans and untucked collared shirts, the women in very high heels and *very* short dresses. Some of the women are as close to naked as you can get and still be technically wearing a garment. I'm guessing they're going to get in.

Michelle and I are definitely the oldest people here. I, personally, am older than the Fontainebleau Hotel. We don't fit in with the LIV crowd at all. If we were to attempt to get into LIV via the standard route—getting in line and trying to make eye contact with the doorman in hopes that he picks us—it would not go well. Years from now, clubgoers would be stepping over our mummified bodies, which would be lying on the marble Fontainebleau lobby floor, our eyeless sockets still aimed hopefully in the direction of the doorman.

So we're not getting in that way. But we are getting in, because I called my friend and *Miami Herald* colleague Lesley Abravanel. She covers Miami nightlife for the *Herald* and is a savvy observer of both the New York and Miami club scenes. I asked her if she could get me into LIV, and she contacted David Grutman, who is the owner of LIV and a Miami nightlife god. He connected me with one of his employees, who goes by the moniker Purple.

Purple sent me a text asking when I planned to get to the Fontainebleau and I answered 11:30. In fact, that is way past my bedtime; I picked a late hour because I wanted to sound like a nightclub sophisticate. Purple responded, quote, "That's extremely early." He explained they were just opening the doors at 11:30. I sheepishly texted back asking if midnight was OK, and Purple, probably realizing that he was dealing with a fossil, said yes.

So here we are, at midnight. I text Purple, who sends out a

polite and large security guy, who escorts Michelle and me past the ropes, into the club and directly to a bar staffed by attractive women bartenders wearing thongs that say "LIV" on the back. The security guy treats us to two cocktails on the house,[1] then leaves. Michelle and I toast each other: Despite being old and unhip and nowhere close to naked, *we're inside LIV.*

Hanging over our heads are speakers the size of Porta-Potties. They're emitting the musical stylings of tonight's celebrity DJ, who is known as Alesso. I am not going to get into my usual rant about "celebrity DJs," a concept that utterly baffles me inasmuch as we're talking about people who are *playing recorded music,* which does not require any more musical talent than operating a microwave oven, in the sense that you could train a reasonably bright Labrador retriever to perform either task, yet somehow these DJs are international celebrities who jet around the world getting huge sums of money to play recorded music THAT THEY DIDN'T EVEN RECORD AND MEANWHILE REAL MUSICIANS WHO CAN PLAY ACTUAL INSTRUMENTS ARE STARVING.

Sorry! It turns out that I cannot stop myself from going

---

1. Thank you, David Grutman. If I ever own a hot nightclub, you are welcome as my guest anytime.

into my usual celebrity-DJ rant. But getting back to Alesso: According to his Wikipedia entry, he "is renowned for his methods of utilizing melodic vibes in his productions." What does that mean, in terms of his actual music, as experienced by the human ear? It means this:

*BOOM BOOM BOOM BOOM BOOM BOOM BOOM*
*BOOM BOOM BOOM BOOM BOOM BOOM BOOM*
*BOOM BOOM BOOM BOOM BOOM BOOM BOOM*
*BOOM BOOM BOOM BOOM BOOM BOOM BOOM*
*BOOM BOOM BOOM BOOM BOOM BOOM BOOM*
*BOOM BOOM BOOM BOOM BOOM BOOM BOOM*
*BOOM BOOM BOOM BOOM BOOM BOOM BOOM*
*BOOM BOOM BOOM BOOM BOOM*

. . . and so on, hour after relentless hour, all night long. It sounds like one long song with no lyrics, mainly consisting of massive bass notes that hit you like invisible punches, causing your sternum to vibrate like a tuning fork and threatening to dislodge your dental fillings.

This genre of music is called Electronic Dance Music, or sometimes Club Music, or sometimes just Loud Unimaginative Absurdly Repetitive Boring Music, because—follow me closely here—it sucks. That is only my opinion, of course; taste in music is subjective. It's possible that you *like* Electronic Dance Music, in which case you are wrong, because it sucks. Fifty years after Elvis, people are still listening to rock and roll; I seriously doubt that fifty years from now people will be using Electronic Dance Music for any purpose other than to tenderize meat.

Michelle and I leave the bar area and walk around LIV. It has two levels: the main dance-floor level and a balcony/ skybox level overlooking the main floor and the DJ booth. On the walls are huge screens, which at the moment are showing a UFC match featuring two women pounding the crap out of each other. The lighting is dramatic, changing constantly, colored laser beams flashing everywhere.

The place is absolutely packed. The crowd looks to be about equally divided between men and women; some of the women are wearing even less clothing than the women outside trying to get in. It feels exciting in here—all the noise and the lights and attractive young people jammed together. It's difficult to talk over the *BOOM*s, so a lot of people are mainly standing around, looking at all the other people standing around. When you get right down to it, there's a lot of standing around going on. But it *feels* exciting.

Michelle and I finish our drinks and move out onto the dance floor, which is jammed with people, some standing around watching DJ Alesso play prerecorded music, some dancing in the modern electronic-dance style, which consists of bouncing up and down in place. In an effort to show these whippersnappers how we used to cut the rug back in the day, I perform a series of classic dance moves from my era, including the Twist, the Jerk and the Mashed Potato. Michelle, embarrassed, makes me stop. This is probably a good thing. LIV has a reputation for trendiness to uphold; the bouncers would probably throw you out if they caught you doing the Mashed Potato. *Especially* to the melodic vibes of DJ Alesso.

While we're out on the floor, a group of club employees emerge from somewhere and make their way through the crowd onto the dance floor. Over their heads they're holding

various illuminated objects: a LIV sign, some champagne bottles with electric candles stuck in the necks and an American Express sign. The employees parade around the dance floor, rhythmically thrusting these objects into the air. It's a living commercial! The message is: *Let's party with abandon! We can charge our alcohol purchases on American Express!*

Michelle and I make our way off the dance floor to one of the bars, where I purchase a smallish rum and coke in a plastic cup for $20. We then head upstairs to get an overhead view of the crowd in front of the DJ booth. I take a picture, but the quality is poor. It's hard to take a good picture when the room is dark and your body is being pummeled by violent bass notes.

At the lower right of this picture, manning the turntables, is DJ Alesso. At least I assume that's who it is. It could also be the lieutenant governor of Montana. There is no way to tell.

After an hour and a half of listening to *BOOM BOOM BOOM* and watching attractive young people stand around, Michelle and I decide to leave. It's getting near 2 a.m., but the Fontainebleau lobby still contains quite a few people standing around hoping to get into LIV. I'm tempted to tell them: "Hey, if you get inside, you'll just be standing around; it's a *lot* cheaper to continue standing around out here." But I have embarrassed Michelle enough already.

We retrieve our car from the Fontainebleau valet ($25) and head home. En route, we stop at an outdoor café in Co-

conut Grove, where we eat cheeseburgers at 2:30 a.m. This is the wildest night we have had in at least a decade.

Talking over the evening, we decide that, except for the music—which, for the record, sucks—we enjoyed ourselves at LIV. It's a fascinating scene and I would recommend it as a one-time experience, even for older people. So if you're ever in the Miami Beach area on a Saturday night, put on your hottest outfit, head over to the Fontainebleau around midnight, get into the line and do your best to impress the doorman. Who knows? Maybe you'll get lucky!

Take at least a year's supply of jerky.

# KEY WEST

It's a lovely bright-blue-sky Wednesday morning in March, and I'm driving on the most spectacular road in Florida, Route 1, the famed Overseas Highway, which hops from key to key for 113 miles. To my left is the Atlantic Ocean; to my right is the Gulf of Mexico. Also to my right is my friend George Pallas, who will be my wingman on this expedition to Key West, the end of the road, the most flamboyant, decadent, debauched and pungent place in Florida.

Key West is Florida's Florida—the place way down at the bottom where the weirdest of the weird end up; the place where the abnormal is normal. Down there, it feels like there's one bar for every three residents, although the actual ratio is probably more like one to four. Key West is the home of Fantasy Fest, a Halloween-week event that could also be called People Walking Around Stark Naked Except for Body Paint. On any given night, Key West's main party drag, lower Duval Street, makes Bourbon Street look like Sesame Street. It has a distinct scent—warm and sticky ocean air mixed with stale beer, Harley exhaust and cigar fumes, accented with a whiff of vomit, a dash of urine and maybe some other fluids. If it's possible to catch an STD just from breathing, lower Duval Street is where it would happen.

In short, it is a fun town. And George is the perfect companion for an evening there, because he's a fun guy *and* a criminal defense lawyer. Also he knows and loves Key West. He owns a bunch of properties there, and he'll use any excuse to visit. When I asked him if he'd be up for a guys' night out on Duval Street, he was all for it. For the record, neither his wife nor mine was thrilled.

We arrive at George's house in the early afternoon. Realizing that we will be visiting many bars in the hours ahead, we decide to prepare, physically and mentally, by drinking some cold refreshing beers. George then gets out a couple of bicycles. He has defended many DUI cases and is a big fan of using bikes for transportation. He has customized his bike with high motorcycle-style "ape hanger" handlebars and a small sound system blaring music. You may think this sounds silly, a grown man riding around on such a bike, but I guarantee you would not say this to George in person. He is a large bald man, and although he's a thoughtful, intelligent person and skilled attorney, he looks like a guy who comes around to your house and persuades you to pay your gambling debt by hitting you on the head with your own femur.

The bike George gives me to ride is far less manly; in fact, it is a lady's bike. But I'm fine with it, because (a) I'm with

George, and (b) this is exactly the kind of thing about which nobody in Key West gives a shit.

With reggae pulsing out of George's bike speakers, we set off pedaling down Duval Street, which is starting to get lively, tourists drifting in and out of the bars and stores selling T-shirts that it's hard to imagine any tourist actually wearing back home (I SHAVED MY BALLS FOR THIS?). At the end of the street, we stop at a food truck and have lunch in the form of excellent fish tacos washed down with cold refreshing beers. Thus fortified, we start making our way back up Duval, bar by bar.

Our first stop is the Hog's Breath Saloon, which is filled with middle-aged tourists drinking beer and listening to a guitar-playing singer who sounds like Jimmy Buffett. These guys are everywhere in Key West, which apparently has a law, rigidly enforced, that says you cannot operate a bar without a guy in shorts and a T-shirt who sounds like Jimmy Buffett singing next to a tip jar. As you wander Duval you hear Buffett-like voices coming from everywhere, singing "Margaritaville," "American Pie," "Piano Man" and other songs that middle-aged beer-drinking tourists like. You do not hear a lot of rap music on Duval.

From the Hog's Breath Saloon we go to Captain Tony's

Saloon, named for the late Tony Tarracino, a legendary Key West character. At various times, Captain Tony was—according to him, anyway—a bootlegger, a gambler, a shrimp boat captain and a gunrunner who worked with the CIA in a plot to overthrow Castro. He was married four times and had fourteen children. Along the way, he became a saloonkeeper; he sold the bar long before he died in 2008, but it still bears his name, and his pictures are all over the walls.

The highlight of Captain Tony's life—again, according to him—was in 1989 when, after multiple tries, he got elected mayor of Key West. He won by thirty-two votes and served one two-year term. As it happened, I interviewed him while he was mayor, for a story I was writing for *The Miami Herald*.

The story involved large colonies of monkeys that were being bred for medical research on two uninhabited mangrove-fringed islands about twenty-five miles from Key West. By 1990, when I wrote about them, the monkey islands had become controversial. Environmentalists were upset about what the monkeys were doing to the mangroves, and animal-rights activists were upset about what researchers were doing to the monkeys. The anti-monkey forces also raised the issue of what would happen if the monkeys—maybe by riding driftwood during a storm—somehow escaped from the islands and got loose in the Keys. As one of the Monroe County commissioners put it at the time, "If you have a hurricane, you're going to blow those monkeys all over the Keys."

For my story, I talked the research people into giving me a tour of the monkey islands, which was fascinating. If you want to see high-tension drama, watch 2,200 screeching, teeth-baring monkeys work out exactly who is going to get how much of the daily allotment of Purina Monkey Chow. It is a process that makes the U.S. Congress look like a calm and thoughtful deliberative body.

I did most of my research for the monkey story in Key West. Among other things, I rented a monkey costume and wore it around to various tourist sites in an effort to determine what impact the presence of monkeys would have on Key West. The answer was: Basically, zero impact. In a town where it is not uncommon to see people walking around naked, nobody's going to get excited about a guy in a monkey suit.

By far the highlight of my research was my interview with Mayor Tarracino. I thought I had an appointment, but when I went to City Hall, there was no one around the mayor's office and the mayor's door was closed. Just when I was about to knock, the door opened and there was Tony. His office was dark and he was blinking like a man who just woke up.

"Hey!" he said, turning on the lights and inviting me into his office.

"Thanks," I said. "I'm Dave Barry, with *The Miami Herald*, and…"

"Hell yes!" said the mayor. "I know! Dick Barry! Sure!"

"Dave Barry," I said.

"Dave Barry!" he said. "Sure! What the fuck can I do for you?"

So I asked him about the monkey menace, and here, as best as I was able to write it down, was his response, which came out in what sounded like one long sentence:

"Way, way back, Tennessee Williams and I were very close friends. Very close. He was going to Russia, and he asked me to take care of his two monkeys, which were named Creature and Lioness, only because Tennessee was gay, Creature was the female and Lioness was the male. I was supposed to have them for six months, but I had them for years. We kept them in a cage in the bar. They were lovers, but he could never bang her—I guess you can't put this in the newspaper, but I'll tell you anyway—he could never bang her unless I got her excited. I'd make these noises like this (*the mayor makes monkey noises*) and she'd go crazy. She loved it. So one day, Creature, which is the female, died, and Lioness, it was so pathetic, just wouldn't let go of her for days, but we finally got her out of there and buried her, it was a nice ceremony, and Tennessee really felt bad. But we had Lioness for many years. He loved marijuana. That monkey was always high. But one day we came in and he was just lying on his shelf there, and we knew it was all over. Am I talking too fast? And so we buried him, it was beautiful, with a little cross. Tennessee called up—I can't tell you how close he was to them, they always knew when he walked in—and I said, 'Tennessee, he didn't suffer.' But talking about monkeys, they're the most human things in the world, once you get to know them. I'd LOVE to have monkeys in Key West. Key West is an outdoor insane asylum anyway. We just never put up the walls."

That remains my favorite journalism interview of my entire career. Now more than ever, this nation needs men like Captain Tony in leadership roles.

George and I enjoy some cold refreshing beers at Captain Tony's while listening to the entertainment, which consists—prepare to be surprised—of a guitar-playing singer who sounds like Jimmy Buffett. He is singing "American Pie" and the tourists are singing right along.

From Captain Tony's, George and I head across Duval to Sloppy Joe's, which is one of the biggest and most popular bars in Key West. There's a big tourist crowd on hand, drinking beer and listening to the entertainment, which consists of—and this may be the secret to Sloppy Joe's success—*two* guitar-playing guys who sound like Jimmy Buffett.

We listen for a few minutes, then leave. We pause outside the Lazy Gecko bar, where beer-drinking tourists are listening to the sounds of a barbershop quartet.

No, seriously, they're listening to a guitar player who sounds like Jimmy Buffett. We decide to head back across Duval. George opens the door to the Red Garter Saloon and goes in, with me following. It does not occur to me—remember, we have been consuming beers—to wonder why this particular bar, unlike the others, has its door closed.

It's darker inside the Red Garter, as there are no windows. Immediately I notice three unusual things:

1. Although there is music playing, *it does not sound like Jimmy Buffett.*
2. There are naked women in here.
3. THERE ARE WOMEN IN HERE WHO ARE NAKED.

It turns out that George, as my local guide, has decided my Key West research expedition needs to include at least one strip club. The Red Garter is one of a half-dozen such clubs in the city.

In case you're wondering how the local political establishment feels about a strip club operating in the middle of the main tourist area, here's a fact you may find helpful: The owner of the Red Garter is Mick Rossi, who is a Key West city commissioner. Rossi also owns a bar next to the Red Garter called Rick's, where, in 2014, Rossi got into a fight with a tourist over a barstool.

According to the *Miami Herald* account of the fight, the tourist asked a woman at the bar if he could take the stool next to her so an older man in the tourist's party could sit on it. According to the tourist, the woman—who turned out to be Rossi's wife—said it was OK. But when the tourist started to move the stool, a gray-haired man—who turned out to be Rossi—started yelling at him and shoving him. The tourist shoved the man back, and next thing he knew he was on the floor, being held down by a Rick's employee and another man, who turned out to be the manager of the waste management company contracted by the city to handle Key West's garbage. According to the police report, Rossi stated that there was "no way anyone was going to take his wife's stool."

You have to admire a man who defends his wife's stool.

In the end, everybody decided it was just a misunderstanding and no charges were pressed. My point is, the Key

West political establishment is not the kind of political establishment to get its thong in a knot over a strip club.

But getting back to the naked women:

I'm uncomfortable in the Red Garter. I don't frequent strip clubs.

Now, you're probably saying: "*Suuure* you don't! Also, you never inhaled!"

No, I definitely inhaled. There was a stretch in the sixties, roughly 1966 through 1969, when I never *exhaled*. But on those extremely rare occasions when I have found myself, always for solid journalism reasons, in strip clubs, I have been very uncomfortable. So here in the Red Garter I'm trying to look cool, or at least keep my lower jaw from touching my kneecaps, but I am nervous. George starts walking through the club, and, not wanting to be left alone, I follow. We pass a very fit naked woman on a stage, leaning over and talking with a man. She looks up and sees George. She smiles brightly and waves. He waves back.

"Who's that?" I ask George.

"My tenant," says George. "She's a nice kid."

The woman resumes talking with the man and we resume walking, toward what George says is the rear exit of the Red Garter. Suddenly our path is blocked by a woman. She is not naked, but she is wearing a very revealing outfit, which reveals that any given one of her breasts would be visible from the International Space Station. She informs us that we can't get out by the back way.

"But you could have a nice lap dance back there," she says.

George and I—both of whom are, for the record, happily married to beautiful sexy women who may very well read this book—politely decline and turn back around. As we pass George's tenant, she again smiles and waves, the friendly way you might wave at a neighbor you see in the supermarket, except, as I believe I have noted, she is naked.

We exit the Red Garter into the afternoon glare and cross back over Duval to a bar called Irish Kevin's, where we drink cold refreshing Irish beers and listen for a while to the guitar player, who is not Irish and who, in fact, sounds like Jimmy Buffett. From there we proceed to the Smokin' Tuna Saloon, which, at the moment, has no musical entertainment but does have a signature drink called the Smokin' Woo Woo. We decide to stick with beer.

We then proceed up Duval to the Bull and Whistle, which has bars on the first and second floors. George informs me that we're going to a third bar, on the rooftop, called the Garden of Eden. This time I know what we're getting into: The Garden of Eden, as the sign outside clearly states, is a clothing-optional bar.

We climb the stairs, and just before the door to the rooftop we encounter a less-inviting sign informing us, among
other things, that we cannot use our cell phones or have sex

on the premises, and that if we try to capture or send images, the Garden of Eden reserves the right to destroy our devices.

We open the door and enter and instantly my eyeballs are struck with great violence by the sight of two people who are extremely naked, but not in a good way. These are two men in their fifties or sixties, lying on lounge chairs positioned so that they face the bar entrance. These are not fit individuals. These are two saggy old exhibitionists, and they are lying with their legs spread apart. I will not go into detail about the vista they are presenting except to say that if you were to capture this image, the Garden of Eden would not have to destroy your device because it would spontaneously explode.

Averting my eyes, I head for the bar, where a group of men are clustered around a topless, tattooed middle-aged woman. She appears to be with one of the men—he has his arm around her shoulders—but she's chatting jovially with the others. They are discussing her tattoos, which are conveniently located in her bosom region, so they're basically just sitting around ogling her, which of course is why she's there.

I purchase two cold refreshing beers. George makes the observation—we've all made it—that so often the people who want you to see them naked are not the people that *you* want to see naked. We decide to move down one flight of stairs and finish our beers in the bar directly below, which is not clothing-optional. We sit on the balcony overlooking Duval, watching the passing parade. A herd of Harley riders the size of full-grown manatees rumbles past, tailpipes blatting.

A few seats down from us on the balcony is a guy drinking a cocktail. After a couple of minutes, a middle-aged couple—the man in shorts and a T-shirt; the woman in a sundress—sits down next to him. The woman asks the cocktail-drinking man if he will take their picture. He says sure, and she hands him a phone. The couple faces the man, which means they are also facing George and me. The woman is sitting on a stool and the man is standing behind her, his hands on her shoulders. They are both smiling for the photo. As the cocktail-drinking man holds up the phone to take the picture, the woman opens her legs wide. I have an excellent view, and can state for a fact that the woman is not wearing any under-wear, nor is she a big believer in intimate personal grooming.

The man takes the photo. The couple thanks him and leaves.

"Did you see that?" I ask George.

"See what?" he says. He missed it. I ask the cocktail-drinking man if he saw it. He says he didn't; he was concen-trating on pressing the right part of the camera screen. So

I'm the only one who saw it. But I definitely saw it. I wonder if this was a spur-of-the-moment decision by the woman, inspired by Key West, or something the couple does everywhere, to create a special photo souvenir. ("And here we are at the Grand Canyon!")

George and I finish our beers and retrieve our bicycles, which, miraculously, we are still able to ride. We pedal to the Green Parrot Bar ("A Sunny Place for Shady People"). We're off Duval now; the crowd is more local, and, at the moment, there is no Buffett-like singer. We enjoy a couple of cold refreshing beers and pedal onward to the 801 Bourbon Bar, which has a cabaret show upstairs in the evening but is pretty quiet at the moment. We order a couple of cold refreshing beers. George asks the bartender about the show; the bartender gives him a postcard with more information and photos of the dancers.

"They're gorgeous," says George.

"They're all guys," says the bartender.

"I know," says George. "Amazing."

I assume it goes without saying that Key West has a major drag scene.

We get back onto our bicycles and pedal onward. This time our destination is not a bar: It is the old Key West fire station, which is now a fire-department museum. We're here to pay homage to a near-mythical Key West figure, a man who ranks right up there in island lore with Captain Tony. I refer to the city's legendary former fire chief, Bum Farto.

Yes: Bum Farto.

Joseph "Bum" Farto was born in Key West on July 3, 1919.[1] He was named fire chief in 1964. He wore rose-tinted glasses and his license plate said EL JEFE. In the 1970s, when there was a lot of drug-dealing going on in Key West, Bum got involved, sometimes selling drugs *from the fire station*. He was arrested in 1975, as part of an investigation called Operation Conch, and in 1976 he was convicted of selling marijuana and cocaine. The mayor at the time, Charles "Sonny" McCoy, said: "This is a very sad day for Key West. It was disappointing to hear these things were actually being done on city property."

(That quote reminds me of Captain Renault's line in *Casablanca*: "I am shocked, shocked to find that gambling is going on in here!")

Three days after his conviction, Bum told his wife he had a meeting in Miami. Then he disappeared. For good. He has not been seen since. For a while, T-shirts that said WHERE IS BUM FARTO? were hot sellers in Key West, but those are

---

1. July 3 is also my birthday. Coincidence? I think not.

scarce now. There's one on display in the firehouse museum, along with Bum's desk and some of his possessions. So the spirit of Bum lives on.

George and I spend a few minutes at the firehouse, burping reflectively, then pedal on back to George's house. We change into warmer clothing—the sun's going down—and prepare ourselves for the evening ahead with some cold refreshing beer.

We set out again, heading back to Duval. We stop briefly outside the Aqua Nightclub, where George takes my picture

with one of the drag performers, who is outside drumming up business and who could play offensive tackle for the Kansas City Chiefs.

We pedal back to lower Duval. We eat at a Thai restaurant that has a sign asking us to please not feed the chickens. There are wild chickens roaming everywhere in Key West; you hear roosters crowing all the time. Some people find the chickens charming, others think they're a noisy nuisance, even a health menace. The attitude of the chickens is *Hey, we're here. What are you gonna do about it?* The answer, this being Key West, is: Nothing.

We leave the restaurant and pause outside Sloppy Joe's, where two guys who sound like Jimmy Buffett—they could be the same two as before, or different ones, there is no way to tell—are leading the tourist crowd in a sing-along. The crowd's part of the song is to yell "FUCK YOU!" The crowd yells this happily.

From there, we head back over to the Hog's Breath, where the entertainment is now a guitar-playing guy and a woman singer *who sounds nothing at all like Jimmy Buffett.* I am tempted to summon the authorities, but I'm pretty sure that Key West *has* no authorities.

We proceed to Durty Harry's, a bar that's part of the entertainment complex owned by the city commissioner who got into a fight with a tourist while defending his wife's stool. Spring Break is under way and the complex is packed with college students. We pay a $5 cover charge and go inside. We drink a couple of cold refreshing beers and listen to the musical entertainment, which is a rock band, the Durtbags, who also sound nothing like Jimmy Buffett. We are the oldest people in there by at least 150 years.

After a while we return to our bikes and pedal over once again to the Green Parrot, which is also packed. The musical entertainment is Cold Hard Cash, a Johnny Cash tribute band. We have now gone to three non-Buffett bars in a row. It's as if the whole world is spinning out of control.

We have what will turn out to be our final cold refreshing beers of the night, then get back on our bikes and wobble home, passing carousing clots of tourists, transvestites, Harley dudes, college students, etc. Also the occasional chicken. It has been a long day, but, at the same time, it has been spectacularly unproductive. A perfect Key West day. I am asleep within seconds.

I awaken the next morning to the sound of roosters crowing and tiny men using jackhammers to break out from inside my skull. George and I need to get back to Miami; we have obligations, and we need to arrange for liver transplants. But before we leave Key West, in the interest of journalism balance, I want to interview one of George's tenants. No, not the woman from the Red Garter. You wish. This tenant is Ed Krane and he's running for mayor.

Krane publishes an online arts and entertainment newsletter called *The Blast,* which is rich with information about Key West's many cultural goings-on. Despite the impression you may have gotten from this chapter, Key West is not just people getting drunk and/or naked. There's also a vibrant cultural scene—art galleries, literary events, music, dance, theater and more—although these things are generally overlooked by uncultured lowlifes such as I.

Ed Krane is a big promoter of the cultural scene, which is partly why he's running for mayor. Our interview takes place on a patio behind George's house. Krane, a trim, boyish man of sixty-three, is wearing jeans and a T-shirt that says ED KRANE FOR MAYOR.

Krane is originally from New York. He's had a number of careers, including selling computers and managing hotels. He also managed nightclubs, and in the eighties was special-events director at the Palladium, the nightclub owned by Steve Rubell and Ian Schrager. He moved to Florida in the nineties and has lived in the Keys for over a decade. He has two opponents for the mayor job: the incumbent, Craig Cates, who's a retired powerboat racer and auto-parts store owner, and Randy Becker, who's a Unitarian Universalist minister.

Krane hands me a campaign flyer listing "some of my platforms." These include:

> Insure that Key West is known for more than our great night life and partying; with major focus on insuring promotion of the arts.
>
> Clean up areas including Duval Street.

I ask him if cleaning up Duval wouldn't hurt the Key West economy, seeing as how the businesses there employ bartenders, waiters, cooks and literally thousands of singers who sound like Jimmy Buffett.

"I don't mean clean it up emotionally," says Krane. "I mean clean it up physically. It's disgusting." He proposes, among other things, to "spruce it up with plants and flowers." He says he still wants fun-seekers to come to Duval, but "we also need to market to people who appreciate the arts. We need both. Key West should be known for its cultural history."

I wish him well with his campaign, but I am doubtful. I

think the main result of putting plants and flowers on Duval would be that people would see them as a handy place to urinate. For most visitors, Key West is a party town. That's its heritage. I don't think it will change much. And, to be honest, I don't want it to.

It's another nice day, so I put the convertible top down for the drive back to Miami on the Overseas Highway. En route, George gets an email on his phone from a friend, sending him a link to a *Miami Herald* story about an incident that took place in Key West last night, while we were cruising around. George reads me the story, which begins:

"'A retired Massachusetts lawyer vowed to make a citizen's arrest on Wednesday against a Key West stripper when she would not have sex with him or return money he paid her, according to police.'"

This happened at a club called Living Dolls. The police report says that the lawyer became "enraged" when an officer refused to help him get his money back. He told the officer he'd return later to make a citizen's arrest, then finally "stormed off with an unsatisfied attitude."

It occurs to me that this incident will probably be viewed as another one of those only-in-Florida stories—*Retired Lawyer Wants to Make Citizen's Arrest on Stripper*—that cause the rest of America to ask, "What is WRONG with you people down there?" But as I noted way back in the Introduction to this book, a lot of those stories—like this one—involve people who came here from somewhere else. They keep coming and coming, because it's warm, because it's wild, because it's weird, because whatever. People keep coming to Florida, and things keep *happening* here.

And I love it.

That's what I'm thinking as George and I motor toward Miami, with the sun glinting off the water on both sides. *I love this crazy state.* I loved it before, but now, having traveled around researching this book, I love it even more.

If you've never been down here, you should check it out sometime. Plan to stay a while, because there's more—*much more*—to see than just what's in this book. Get in a car and drive around. See the sights and view the vistas, the water, the sky. Watch the critters, and the people. Taste the flavors, smell the aromas, listen to the sounds, feel the vibes. Maybe have a few cold refreshing beers.

Take your time. It's a big place.

And if you can't figure out how to leave: Welcome home.

# ACKNOWLEDGMENTS

I thank Tim Dorsey, who knows more about Florida weirdness than anybody, for steering me to some of the places I visited in researching this book. I thank Jeff Whichello for his expertise on the dwindling but defiant community of Ochopee. I thank my smart and funny colleague Lesley Abravanel for enabling me to become the oldest living human ever to get into LIV. Thanks also to my cousin-in-law Ron Ungerman, who is always up for an adventure, even if it involves machine guns. And thanks to my friend George Pallas for sacrificing his time and brain cells to spend a day and night with me attempting to drink all the beer in Key West. We failed, but, dammit, we tried.

As always I am grateful to my amazing assistant, Judi Smith; any mistakes in this book are totally her fault. Thanks to my fierce yet loving agent, Amy Berkower, who should be running the country; and to my editor and literary mentor, the avuncular yet studly Neil Nyren.

I thank my amazing wife, Michelle Kaufman, for letting me traipse around Florida researching this book, and for not getting mad when all I brought her back was a sponge.

Finally, I thank my readers, who keep me from going sane.